Spring Garden

Spring Garden

NEW AND SELECTED POEMS BY

Fred Chappell

LOUISIANA STATE UNIVERSITY PRESS
BATON ROUGE AND LONDON

1995

04 03 02 01 00 99 98 97 96 95   5 4 3 2 1

Designer: Amanda McDonald Key
Typeface: text, Granjon; display, Old English and Granjon
Typesetter: Impressions
Printer and binder: Thomson–Shore, Inc.

Library of Congress Cataloging-in-Publication Data

Chappell, Fred, 1936–
      Spring garden : new and selected poems / by Fred Chappell.
      p.   cm.
      ISBN 0–8071–1948–2 (cl : alk. paper). — ISBN 0–8071–1949–0 (pbk :
alk. paper)
      I. Title.
PS3553.H298S69   1995
811'.54—dc20   95–22425
                                                          CIP

Poems selected herein appeared, sometimes in slightly different form, in volumes previously published by Louisiana State University Press as follows: from *The World Between the Eyes* (1971), "Fast Ball," "The Fields" (originally "The Farm"), "Heath at Eight: New Drum Set," "Heath at Two: Learning to Talk," "Junk Ball," "Seated Figure," "Spitballer," "Strike Zone," and "Third Base Coach"; from *River* (1975), "My Grandmother Washes Her Feet"; from *Earthsleep* (1980), "Susan's Morning Dream of Her Garden"; from *Source* (1985), "Abandoned Schoolhouse on Long Branch," "Child in the Fog," "Humility," "Latencies," "Message," "Narcissus and Echo," "Nocturne," "A Prayer for the Mountains," "Recovery of Sexual Desire After a Bad Cold," "The Story," "Transmogrification of the Diva," and "The Virtues"; from *First and Last Words* (1989), "Afternoons with Allen," "Dipperful," "The Garden," "How the Job Gets Done," "Literature," "Meanwhile," "My Hand Placed on a Rubens Drawing," "An Old Mountain Woman Reading the Book of Job," "Patience," "Pierrot Escapes," "The Reader," "Remodeling the Hermit's Cabin," "Scarecrow Colloquy," "Score," "Slow Harbor," "Teller," "Visitation," and "Voyagers"; and from *C* (1993), "Ave atque Vale," "The Epigrammatist," "Epitaph: Lydia," "A Glorious Twilight," "The Good Life" (originally "How to Do It"), "Grace Before Meat," "Honeysuckle," "I Love You," "In the Garden," "Literary Critic" (and "Another" and "Another"), "Marigold," "Nettle," "No Defense," "Overheard in the Tea Room," "Rejoinder," "Rx," "Satire," "Sex Manual," "The Stories," "Threads," "The Ubi Sunt Lament of the Beldame Hen" (here incorporated in the general prologue), and "Upon an Amorous Old Couple." The "Epilogue" is forthcoming (1995) in *Image.* New poems in this volume are "Avignon and Afterward," "The Bible of the Unlucky Sailor," "Cathedral," "Dialogue of Naughty and Nice," "Dr. Bones," "The Fated Lovers: A Story," "Fleurs-des-Livres," "Forever Mountain," "The General Prologue," "Going Through Zero to the Other Side," "Moonswarm," "The Presences at Sunset," "(Prologue)," "Rider," "The Rose and Afterward," "The Sea Text," "Some of It," "Tiger in the Field of Flame Grass," "The Tipsy Diva Remembers Pierrot," "The Transformations: A Fairy Tale," "U.S. Porn Queen (Ret.)," "Upon a Confessional Poet," "The Voices," and "The Widow."

For my sister Rebecca

Contents

The General Prologue

This morning in the wellspring month of May
Let's take our coffee out beneath the sky,
Observe the laurel blooming contentedly,
And make our plans for this Memorial Day.
The year's at spring, but I no longer am;
Decades have mounted, as we were told they would;
The time has come when there's but little time
To write daft poems and speculate on God.

The day has come for us to winnow through
The pages of my crossgrain poetry books,
Searching for any line at all that looks
Suitable for a volume Old and New.
A poet loves a simple irony,
And that we're harvesting these poems in spring
Is a theme of Robert Herrick's poetry
And one that Ronsard took delight to sing.

This same Ronsard invited his friend Jamyn
To wander in the garden and collect
Herbs for a salad, careful to select
The healthful ones that might sustain a man
Who'd suffered quartan fevers, disastrous love,
The whims of kings and the unhappy fate
Of being called by music when he'd gone deaf
To tune his sonnets to an antique lute.

Forgive my mention of the Renaissance.
Those poets are not popular nowadays;
They sang too much of love, rained fulsome praise
On any portly bishop or spendthrift prince,
Were rarely ever politically correct,
Surrendered to the sweet pursuit of pleasure,
Tippled till they could hardly walk erect,
And—worst of all!—wrote poems in rhyme and measure.

They are the figures, though, that seem to me
Embodiments of the purest soul of song,
Simulacra of Idea flung
Into being by momentous energy

That animates each penstroke of their work.
—Not a current fancy, I'm afraid,
In these last years of the latest age gone dark,
But one in which I take imprudent pride.

Because by now poetic reputation
Hardly excites me. I've done the best I could
With what I had. Whether the lines are good
Or dismal, I stand behind their procreation
And wrote more of them than ever I expected,
Forfeiting rare time for the sake of art.
I've heaped this volume up, *New and Selected*—
Which marks me as a certified Old Fart.

So let us gather, Susan, what we can find
In my weedy garden of verse that might compose
A salad, poems not tough with cellulose
Or soft with rot or nothing but hollow rind.
We seek out lines still green and with some savor,
A stanza here and there with a bouquet
Of sunlight, humus, rain, the virid flavor
Of fresh-turned earth, perfume of new-mown hay.

That they'll be hard to come by, I understand.
I feel, as any poet must, regret
I fell below the standards that I set
Almost every time I put my hand
To verse—but not because I didn't try
To write the best I could day after day.
And now, as Ronsard says, my youth's gone by
Too soon, "Ma douce jouvance est passée":

    My pliant youthfulness is gone,
        My stamina all broken down,
        My teeth are black, and white my head,
        My heart is weak, my nerves are shot
        And through my veins runs nothing but
        Icy water instead of blood.

    Adieu to poetry, adieu
        To all the girls that are and were;
        Goodbye, I feel the end come on.
        Three joys only of younger days

Remain with me as constancies:
My bed, my fire, my glass of wine.

Numerous years and numberless days
Weigh me down with illnesses,
Fears gnaw my every hope;
Though I fly onward like the wind
Every time I glance behind
I find that Death is catching up.

This Death, who means to take my hand
And lead me to an unknown land,
Whose final purpose I cannot learn,
Holds that door open through which we go
To some dark land beyond, below,
The door admitting no return.

—But this chanson is just a little grimmer
Than I'd recalled. There may be years to come
With promise almost as pleasing as our past time
Whose blaze begins to dwindle to a glimmer.
I am precipitate to mourn so soon;
There will be other springs, and winters too,
Before the whisper-snow descends upon
The stone that marks our long velvet curfew.

Carpe diem is till a proper theme
For us; it's more important to seize the day
When there are fewer left. The common clay
Of time we'll burn with our uncommon flame
Into a shape expressive, however small,
However marred, of all our life together.
There's still a bit of summer before the fall—
So here's that gay rondeau of Maytime weather:

Summer has ordered his footmen in
To freshen his chateau cheerfully,
To brighten up his tapestry
With flowers and grass all sweet and green.
    Thick shag carpets are spread out when
On the verdure he passes by;
Summer has ordered his footmen in

To freshen his chateau cheerfully.
    Our spirits are alive again
That had been frozen in ennui.
Winter, say a short goodbye,
There's not one reason you should remain:
Summer has ordered his footmen in.

In the Garden

That rondeau by the Duke of Orléans
Serves as antefoyer to the first section
Of our severe and much-debated selection,
Which shall begin by ringing changes on
The subject of gardens, a theme that occupies
The both of us, but me more comfortably
Since I don't weed or water, prune or prize
Up rocks, but only write my poetry

And watch my Susan at her charming labors
With rhododendron and anemone,
Virginia creeper and liriope,
And white azaleas that startle our neighbors
With their cool spectral twilight lantern-shine.
The flowers I pretend to cultivate
Are metaphorical: line after line
Whereon critics, like passing collies, micturate.

Each kind of toil has its advantages.
Yours results in pleasure the body takes
With all its senses, suave murmur that speaks
To spirit, musical in every breeze.
My dry pressed flowers the neighbors never see,
Since they're in books and books are rarely read,
Or if they are, they're rarely poetry
By Dabney, Rodney, Betty, Kay, or Fred.

Real enough, but half-imaginary,
This garden we tend together shall provide
Ingredients for a salad like Ronsard made,
Quite practical and yet quite visionary.
Lettuce we'll have, that symbol of well-being;
And one strange herb that promotes fantasies
Blithe or ominous, new ways of seeing;
And tastes that call back cherished memories.

Epigrams shall be our watercress;
Fern seed to make ourselves invisible
In order to observe the sorrowful
Or happy lives of others, their taut distress,

Pensive repose, deft skills, or careless chatter.
And, most important, herbs that urge to love
We'll have in plenty, for love's the serious matter
We play upon in our enchanted grove.

So let us wander, Susan, the greenery
You've planned and planted, sprayed and spaded, tended
Season-long and valiantly defended
Against the grubs and mites such scenery
Delectably attracts. What's salad for us
Is salad too for the insect universe.
In our garden let's celebrate the rose,
As Jean de Baïf counseled in his verse:

> The rose is the loveliest kind of bloom
> If we gather it in time.
> See it luminous with dawn?
> By this evening it will be gone.

Susan's Morning Dream of Her Garden

The way a tree climbs down into the earth,
and earth to stop its drifting like a bed
seizes the cloudmass roots;

and into ground lean the lonely and elaborate dead
as powdery as sleet,
burbling to each other always,

a full Four Hundred of juicy talkers; the way
the headstrong sunflower, the boxwood and Harpwoof,
the Spragglewort, moondime and Dusty Miller, the pansies

with their Pekinese faces, and grimbleweed lift out
and up in light their informal forms,
pistil and petal half-shadow:

is the way my hand goes into the dirt.
Or is it flesh I enter?
My own? Or lubberhubby's lying this plot with me?

Haho. He. He is loose in sleep
and musical as a horse, goeth as a zinnia
brave to daybreak and casts a watershaped snore.

Why are men so toady, tell me, touching
the moss and root? I'll tend me well my contrary garden.
Now my rows of queenly corn erupt to cadenza;

and the cabbages unfurl
outward and inward like sentences of Proust,
the sweet rose invites her oriental suitors

iridescent in green and oil, and yonder my neat row
of bones blossoms mouths of marrow,
yet I am not replete or reconciled.

Garden, garden, will you not grow for me
a salon full of billets-doux and turtledoves?
Garden, garden, green tureen,

Will you not put me forth the olden ladies upsidedown
in their hooped skirts like the bells of lilies,
their clapper legs chiming sentimental songs?

I long to belong to
the chipper elegance, those centuries where
the hand of man has never said an ugly word.

I own an antique plate in which I see
a little garden with a swing, a young girl
in the swing, tra-la, beset with birds of every hue,

troo-loo.
The swing girl's face is a mint of pale pink roses.
In the garden I grow I'm the girl in the swing, ting-a-ling.

And I rise and rise in my swing through the globe
of green leaves giddy till I become
a rose-pink butterfly with arms of eyes.

We whirl, my garden and I, until
the minuet boils, the sun
and moon and lawn and tree become a waltzing sea,

a jiggy river of green green green.
Hurl-whorl green into which we roll
as down a well of hay.

I sing as high and clear-O as a finch
in a yellow-green willow tree,
transparent and vivid as dragonflies.

I'd be a fool, a woman's a fool, to be drawn back
into the waking world,
all dinky clutter and dirty bathtub.

You won't catch me yet, New Day, I'm snugging
deeper in the hideaway of dream,
I'm burrowing like a roly-poly whistlepig

into the green earthflesh of sleep, keep
your tarnished-silver fingers, Sun, off my bright hair,
off my pillow, my mellow wallow.

I'm diving to a door I sense below,
a door as yellow with catlight as the eye of an owl,
that opens truly into the garden

on my antique plate and can draw
my waking body in and there no one
can draw me out again. No use, you-all,

I'm gone beyond your smirch, you can't
get in, I'm the slattern in the pattern.
Admire, admire!

The Garden

The garden is a book about the gardener.

His thoughts, set down in vivid greenery,
The white light and the gold light nourish.
Firm sentences of grapevine, boxwood paragraphs,
End-stops of peonies and chrysanthemums,
Cut drowsy shadows from the afternoon.

Out of their hiding places the humid twilight
Lures the stars. The perfumes of the grass
Draw like cool curtains across the mind
And what the mind is certain it is certain of.

So that the twilight fragrances are clearly audible,
The garden stroking the senses with slow roses.
Bats ramble overhead, tacking from star
To early star as if putting in at ports of call.
And then the Chinese lantern is lit as it was in childhood,
As central in that place as an island lighthouse.

The gardener is a book about his garden.
He walks among these leaves as easy as morning
Come to scatter its robins and tender noises.
As the plants inhale the morning and its cool light,
The book is open once again that was never shut.
What now we do not know we shall never know.

Nettle

I have teeth
Beneath;
And a flower too
Of cool blue
With a center star
Of yellow sheath.

As common as air,
Startling as fire.

Marigold

Daystar crinkled
Upon the stream.
Flower of sultry dream
Where the bee twinkled.

Honeysuckle

Granted by right divine,
I say, *this field is mine!*

The Fields

The hay, the men, are roaring on the hill.
July muzzy and itchy in the fields,
Sunlight opens its mouth on the tractor's drone,
Bumblebees like thumbs in the bolls of red clover.
Summer within the field, unsparing fountain
Of heat and raw savor.
               The men redden and sweat,
Their torsos flash, the talk and the laughing jet up cool,
Single cool sound in the saffron air, air like a woolen cloak.
The land lies open, at the mercy of the trembling sun.
One cloud drives east; the cattle plunder the brackish pools,
Black flies fumble on their hides.
They chew, observe the hour with incurious eye.

Mouths agape, the men gulp fierce breath.
If now a breeze could lift the fields!
. . . But their skins cloy with dust. Grin and gouge.
Neck muscles sore, exhaustion laps the bodies,
Their mouths are desperately open, fork-tines feint and plunge.
And then the woman brings the water, the clear jar
Echoing rings of light that flutter on her apron.

Now the wagon is heaped and going away.
Bronze-green hay like a shaggy skirt, the wagon
Halts then sways unsteady to the barn.
Bronze-green tongues of it leap to the sill.
They harry it in and the loft is bulging,
Surfeit beneath the tin roof of sheeted fire.
Mouse-gray pigeons march and croon,
Dipping beaks like shards of flower pots.

. . . The hill bare now, blackbirds swoop in a sudden net,
Scatter like pepper specks. The men, those shouts of flesh,
Gone home to the wash basin, to the glowing table.
Slow dark: the mountains empurple and encroach.

Hay all in, tobacco now and corn
As the ground sleeps and cools, the barns huddle
At twilight, bats in the starry dusk like pendulums.
Goldenrod indolent, blue moonlets of chicory,

Queen Anne's lace precise as the first stars of frost.
Ponds grimace and show their teeth
As the winds tug the westward mountains.

The land, clenched shut.

Trees thrash, noble and naked wrestlers,
Clouds mass within and beneath the heavy winds.
The shining birds go away, but quail and bobwhite
Keep the drying pasture. Thistle spends its silver,
Frost drives through rind and pith.

                             The brittle season:
Crash crash of leaves in seemly groves;
Austerity of alders;
Blue grapes;
Last glimmer of crickets.

Then winter in the hearth.
The sizzling oak joint snaps like cap pistols
And the smoke rolls generous under the sky.
The grandaddy snorts and nods;
His chessboard idles while whiskey nudges his elbow.
All the rooms grow smaller, creak creak
The timbers mutter. House tightens and the roof howls.
Ice like cheesecloth on the still water;
Glass needles in the ground.
Rattles, clinks;
Clear rime.

The stupor of cold wide stars.

And in the narrowed fields the wind from dead north
Mauling the cattle together, furrowing hides
Red and white, sifts into the creases
First snow like moss. They moan at the gate,
Turning the whited eye. Spaces between boards
Ice-crusted, the barns let the blow in.
Sleet piddles the ridged roofs.
The sky is volumes of smeary grays, and flesh
Pinches and rasps, the skin chill and reluctant.

First deep snow then, and the sun blind on it,
Edges depart the customary to reveal their truth.

Nothing is stark. The light enlarges
Such a fearful blue the mind burns with pain,
Body feels evanescent as mist.
                                    Night closes over,
Deep crucible merciless and songless.
The land creeps to star-marge,
Horizon cluttered with light,
                    indifferent emblem of eternity.

Nothing will move but the whisperless wheel of sky:

Axis that fixes and orders revolves on a hub of ice:

The houses burrow deeper and deeper.

The world: locked bone.

Patience

a prologue to *The Georgics*

1
An early summer evening.
                        The broad homophony
Of the hive of stars immerses the dark porches where
The farmers muse. It seems that all the earth there is
Has been taken by the plow, and the hedgy boundaries
Of orchards encroach upon the sea, all the sea
There is, the planet lapped in grateful breathing fields:
Here the labor is, here the finished work.

Night blackens the red ox in his pen, the roan horse
Shines like dust of galaxies: our faithful creatures—
For whom time passing is a patience almost mineral,
Whose sleep this evening folds over like a loamy furrow—
Snort, and settle to the ground like velvet boulders;
And ivy in the night curls up about them bronze.

The farmers and their animals have molded the world
To a shape like some smooth monumental family group,
The father mountains, mother clouds, their progeny meadows
Disposed about them, as if posing for a photograph
To be taken from a silver orbiting spaceship by beings
Like angelic horses, who return to their home world
With pleasant report: *Leave Earth alone, it is at peace.*

2
Always the Poet knew it wasn't so.
                        Total
War throughout the globe, justice and injustice
Confounded, every sort of knavery, the plow
Disused unhonored, the farmer conscripted and his scythe
Straitly misshapen to make a cruel sword.
                        The East
Imbrued, and northern Europe, and all the smaller tribes
Ceaselessly breaking their treaties, and Mars the bully
Savages every field. The shepherd and the herdsman,
Et robustus item curvi moderator aratri,

And the muscular steersman of the crooked plow, are killed,
The cottager mothers flung on the corpses of their children—
As when the horses seize the bit from the chariot-driver
And thunder over the circus barrier into the crowd,
He jerks the useless reins, the car will not respond.

3

Such slaughter, they say, manures the fields of Utopia,
So that the plowman in a sleepier century
Turns up the bones of a legendary Diomedes
And marvels that the land had nourished those giants
Who now have become the subsoil in which the Capitol
Is footed, where the softhanded senators daylong
Argue the townsman's ancient case against the farmer:
He is behind the times, he will never understand.
The decisions there brought back in the form of levies
And soldiers, who look with envious eyes upon this life
They fleer at, guzzling the raw-edged country wine.

But nothing changes. The war grinds over the world and all
Its politics, the soldiers marry the farmers' daughters
And tell their plowman sons about the fight at the Scaean Gate,
And other sanguine braveries the dust has eaten.
Sundown still draws the chickens to their purring roost,
The cow to the milking stall, the farmer to his porch to watch
If the soaring constellations promise rain.

Literature

The girls and flowers keep changing into literature
until that endless languid age arrives
when all the world becomes a picture catalogue of gardens
where men and women play at chess, at love,
and every animal comes gentle to the hand.

Then the spirit must begin once more,
untaming everything that it has tamed,
forgetting all that it has paid in blood,
until the blazoned phrases melt from the vellum
and the gold-leaf initials turn into butterflies
and lift off the pages, climbing into space
to find the hidden planet all wild rose and chicory.

Slow signals are emitted from that far system.
The planet throbs in its orbit like a hive of sleepy bees,
the seasons settle into an undying summer
where poplar leaves slide in the wind
like shoals of rainbow trout nibbling the river.
It is a world prepared for men,

but no one comes, each reader still entranced
by the courtly chronicle of his native world,
the book that murmurs the secret names of lovers.

The Good Life

"Lettuce we'll have, that symbol of well-being":
So I promised in an earlier page,
And we shall have it. In our modern age
It's not a rarity. The ancient saying
That lettuce brings contentment and good health
Has proven true. Lettuce saved the life
Of Augustus Caesar and heaped his doctor's wealth.
It promotes amity and muffles strife;

Requires more calories to eat than it provides
And therefore is the dieter's mainstay;
Diminishes the bitterness of dry
Hot herbs like rocket; its goodness includes
An unctuous partnership with mayonnaise
And a slice of ripe tomato on wholewheat toast;
With oil and lemon is guaranteed to please
Those guests most finicky and their thoughtful host.

Cool lettuce, as writeth Dioscorides
In his *Materia Medica,* translated by
John Goodyear in the seventeenth century,
Doth loosen costive bowels and give them ease,
And Martial wrote an acerbic little poem
Decrying luxury, high on his chart
Of evils he predicted would bring down Rome—
Lettuce served first, instead of as dessert.

Lettuce and the Good Life are conjoined
As complementaries. They're nothing but
Ideas in themselves, yet when they're set
Inside the elegant design we've planned,
Alongside stronger flavors, nobler aims,
With nice particulars that add detail
To emphasize the tenets of our themes,
We find them necessary to the whole.

And this Good Life, as I portray it here,
Consists in steady work and fortitude,
Of worthy books and modest quietude,
Science and art, of noble things that were

And are to be—along with naughtiness
Of the tame domestic sort, and speculation
About the lives of ancients, a friendly glass
Or two: fit objects for proper admiration.

And don't I wish that I had held to these
With stalwart faith and unrelaxing strength
Of will? Of course I do. But life's brief length
Makes infinite room for rash inconstancies.
You can't desire me to confess my sins,
All of them boring, none a thrilling show.
I've fancied that inside this garden fence
Virtue could be easier than we know,

A notion our First Parents might dispute.
Remembering their famous contretemps,
They might point out that place bears little on
A true attainment of moral rectitude.
—And now I see that I've begun to preach,
A nasty habit I work to leave behind.
Let's let the politicians rant and screech
While mellow Statius recalls our theme to mind:

Reluctant winter heads for New England
Regretting the springtime that conquers it;
    The pastures and lakes now shimmer,
        Snowstorms gentled to breezes.

Now every tree is frilly with leafage,
The green that spring returns perennially;
    The birds are singing recitals
        They rehearsed all winter in whispers.

I sit beneath my paper umbrella
Beside our small remodeled pumphouse
    With its cunning drawings of zephyrs
        And refresh myself with verses.

No anxious brokers call to remind me
I'm losing money to rampant inflation;
    Our laurels but nod approval
        When I hit upon a simile.

Grace Before Meat

Bless, O Lord, our daily bread.
Bless those in hunger and in need
Of strength. Bless all who stand in want.
Bless us who pray, bless us who can't.

How the Job Gets Done

A dust of rubble warriors whitens the plain
where the chariots plunged and shattered. The sleep
of bronze and the ceaseless memorial wind
caress those acres like a crop of wheat;

the rivers have carried away the mules flyblown
and bloated, the torn veils of the widows,
the hafts and dented greaves, the portable gods.
Insubordinate Thersites got seven solid years

latrine duty no one is marking now, except
the poet in his garden, laboring to line-end,
then turning back like a sweating plowman to fold
another loamy furrow over the crumbled palaces.

My Hand Placed on a Rubens Drawing

1

It is what it is,
And being what it is, is something more
Than its wrinkle, thumb, and knobble indicate.
The lumpy knuckles, chipped and pitted nails,
Gross pores and ashen stipple of keratin spots,
Little scars with forgotten histories:
My hand no uglier than another man's
Middle-aged, luckless, but not brutal hand,
Expressing a studied inexpressiveness.

So much a part of my world, it is my world
And cannot enter the one the scholars have named
Study of a Woman with Crossed Hands,
A world that Rubens with some thousand strokes
Has set in motion, then has set at rest.

My hand placed on the drawing, that universe
So overflooded with its single dream.
Both worlds intransigeant as never before,
Their transit far and darkling.
                                        Not a shadow
My hand throws on the page; a spirit rises,
Antique and cool, out of the page to touch
My hand. And then recoils. Returns inside
Its nest of scrawlwork, blot, and thoughtful smear.
My unacknowledged hand lifts slowly backward:
I am become alien to myself.

Myself a stranger to myself.
                                        The gods
Affect us in just this way: passing by
Heedlessly, absorbed by what absorbs
Divinities, they tremble the human earth
Like marble temples falling one by one.
They are close enough; it is enough
To think they once created the history,
Unmoving burning star-scarp pitiless,
The history that now rejects my hand.

2

Woman with Crossed Hands

Not the usual Rubens woman.
                                          That is,
Not one of his grand horsy Venuses
Who has donned a robe of opalescent flesh
The way she might step into royal ermine
For the painter's convenience; splendidly clothed
In splendid nudity, big pearly dumpling
Who embodies longing's sleekest fulfillment.
Not one of these.
                              A younger woman. Drifting,
Just now having drifted, into a trance
Of shadowed reverie. Lips barely parted,
The gaze affectionate, fixed upon
Some object the chalk and pencil have left undrawn.
A figure for an Adoration, perhaps,
A quiet figure not less joyful because
Rubens for once is not sounding the whole
Outsized orchestra of Flemish flesh,
The tuba bellies and thighs, kettledrum buttocks,
The pale blonde appogiatura breasts.

She is chamber music, intimate
Though a bit withdrawn, modestly
Intoning her demure contralto line.

She is enchanted. She was going to smile,
And then forgot. Something came over her—
A sybilline moment with a daydream peek
Into a happy future, warm, unhurried,
Maternal, graceful, ripe with joys foreseen.
Her face *incipient;* it will come to blossom,
Some future hour, into a various garden
Of expression: giggles, kisses, dimples, frowns;
She will unveil the smile she forgot to smile.

The hands, however, are an accomplished event;
Like my own hands, they are just what they are.
Graceful but never noble, they tell the story
Of farmer ancestry, staunch country forebears,

And contradict in some small measure the easy
Fine bearing of the head. Thoroughly modeled,
They emerge from the blouse-cuff—cascade of scribble,
Ebullient froth of marking—as Venus rose
Out of the sea-foam whole and ready as sunlight.
The smell of earth about them, undertone
Of cabbage, onion, turnip, and the branmeal loaf.

Rubens sinks the piers of vision deep
Into the earth, secures the billowed gods
And hurtling towers, the saints and babes and heroes—
All that panoply of gleaming triumph—
With her whose hands the paring knife and grater
Have sculpted to simple peace and simple welcome.

3
The ages work toward mastery
Of a single gesture. A torso's twist,
The revelation of a thigh,
White stone corded in a fist:

Fragments that might still add up
To compose a figure of the perfected soul
As it releases from the grip
Of vision that burned to draw it whole.

The Good Life

"Chappell—you who love to jest—
Hear the things that make life blest:
Family money not got by earning;
A fertile farm, a hearthfire burning;
No lawsuits and no formal dress;
A healthy body and a mind at peace;
Friends whom tactful frankness pleases;
Good meals without exotic sauces;
Sober nights that still spark life;
A faithful yet a sexy wife;
Sleep that makes the darkness brief;
Contentment with what you plainly need;
A death not longed for, but without dread."

—Martial

Rejoinder

Now let's even up the score
And tell what things make life a bore:
Sappy girls who kiss and tell;
Televangelists' threats of hell;
Whining chainsaws, mating cats;
Republicans; and Democrats;
Expertly tearful on their knees,
Plushlined senators copping pleas,
Swearing by the Rock of Ages
That they did not molest their pages;
Insurance forms and tax reports;
Flabby jokes and lame retorts;
Do-gooders, jocks, and feminists;
Poems that are merely lists.

Dialogue of Naughty and Nice

Naughty

You skillfully persuade your pantieless wife
Under the table in the bustling restaurant
To raise her skirt. Drolly you drop your knife.
One crisp and musky peek is all you want—
And get—before the starchy maitre d'
Comes to inquire in tones of costly frost
If anything is wrong, Sir? May I assist?
"I've got it under control," you say. Teehee.

Now that's·*adventure,* that's what Naughty is:
The kind of Escapade that Nice would never
Dream of. Stratagems of bright surprise,
Sauces with Tabasco tang, clever
Ballades about the girls who flaunt their glories
In the piquant streets of pink Paree, tales
Of tiddly bishops. *Naughty* are the stories
Told of Chaucer's canny animals.

Nice

But don't you feel, friend Naughty, that your taste
Is questionable? Is that episode
As thoroughly sexy as you make it out?
Doesn't it leave your darling wife red-faced?
There comes a time we find we've done it all,
Or we've imagined it as done, and know
Pleasures keener than Naughty enjoys; and so
We pass it up as being not worthwhile.

I'll tell you what *adventure* is: to breed
A new shade of chrysanthemum, to spot
A rare grosbeak in the familiar glade,
To bake a loaf of bread and break it hot
And smear on yellow butter and cut a square
Of green-veined crumbly Stilton, pour a glass
Of wine—perhaps a Riesling from Alsace—
And finish off with a blushing Anjou pear.

Voyagers

after Vermeer's *The Astronomer*

The scholar and his globe celestial,
His book that names the fixed and ambling stars,
Their ascensions, declinations, appointed seasons:

Hic pinxit. In this dim room that admits no more
Of Delft than its refined gray window-light,
This room that silence studies like a science,

The scholar and his celestial globe commerce.
He turns the globe, he turns the pages, the silver
Little pages that speak in pillars of numbers

Of when the homesick sea captain first glimpsed
Centaurus in the southern latitudes
And wrote the name of it and the lonesome hour.

The dagger coast of Tierra del Fuego
Discloses fjord by fjord itself as the pages
Turn, the scholar and his whirligig

Agree. The oceans after all agree
With what the astronomer tells the stars to do
From his room at Delft with his little silver book.

The Virtues

The vices are always hungry for my hands,
But the virtues stay inside their houses like shy brown thrushes.

I feel their presences
Behind the white clapboard walls with all the tacky gingerbread.

They are strolling the dim cool rooms
In handsewn linen dresses.

Is it vain to hope they will come out
To sweep the walks when I stand beneath the oak across the street?

The virtues are widowed sisters;
No man has been with them for many years.

I believe thay are waiting for cataclysm.
They will open their doors

When perfect ruin has taken down this city,
Will wander the avenues and sift thoughtfully the smoking rubble.

The Garden of Love

At least a score of herbs have got the name
Of being surefire aphrodisiacs.
Believe me, Susan, if there were any facts
To prop these fantasies, those herbs would claim
Prices nearly unimaginable.
To tell the truth, I might invest a few
Loose bucks. Since we've been married for a full
Thirty-five years . . . Well, darling, so might you.

Then let our salad include ingredients
Reputed to warm the cockles of the heart,
Whatever cockles are. Ovid's *Art*
Of Love lists some well-tried expedients,
Both of the herbal and strategic kinds;
Gerard notes three; Dioscorides
And Turner seem to be of different minds;
But not one word from noble Hippocrates.

Even so, it's said that watercress
And chervil, lamb's-quarters, ginseng, shepherd's-purse,
And friendly thyme can take away the curse
Of impotence, and that a fresh-picked mess
Of mustard, radish leaf, and chicory,
Coltsfoot and spurge are swift at conquering
The wealthy widow's cautious timidity.
Yarrow is often called Bad Man's Plaything.

Folklore's a better guide than science when
It's love, amour, and Eros we have in mind.
Perhaps some horny chemistry whiz will find
A potion that makes Don Juan of any man,
But I don't want to know, for I prefer
The billet-doux, the ballad and serenade,
The sentimental valentine; these stir
My feelings. And so does Ronsard's pretty ode:

Darling, let's go and view the rose
That in the early morning dews
Opened its colors to the sun.

It may have lost by twilight time
The scarlet of its pleated bloom,
Its beauty equal to your own.

You see how quickly destructive are
The moments that pile up hour on hour:
Alas, that loveliness is gone!
Dame Nature shows a murderous power
When such a rose cannot endure
At least till vespers from the dawn.

Please believe me, Susan dear,
This present time is your sweetest year;
You flower as if newly sprung.
So gather, gather, while you may—
Unfriendly age is on its way
With its envy of all us young.

How jocund is your plangency, mon vieux!
You have a knack for making dance a gigue
Regrets and sorrows, for caring not a fig
For fame, even that of lucky Pierre.
This is a pose you've borrowed from the Greek
And Latin poets who grew green again
And modern when you tutored them to speak
The brisk French of the region of Gastine.

But love can also be quiet and somber,
Contain a silence that eternity
Cannot dismay, with a trembling certainty
That hour by hour death slides its scythe-shaped umbra
Over the bright albedo of our day
As it brings on its darkness, on and on,
Till not one gleam is left in our long sky—
As in this poem by Emile Verhaeren:

And when you close my eyes upon the light
Give them a lingering kiss. They shall retain
In my last glance that this world shines upon
The love those final hours cannot defeat.

In the steady silence of the candleflame
Read their desolate farewell, then lean
Your beautiful unhappy face close down
And let them take your image to the tomb.

And let me feel, before the end comes on,
You lay your cheek, with a slow liquid sigh,
Beside me on the pillow where I lie
And join our hands on the linen counterpane.

And may it happen after I expire
That I still hold such thought of you that all
Across the world the other dead shall feel
The warmth pulsing from our undimming fire.

The Fated Lovers: A Story

I
Mary Won't Marry

No I'll not marry at all at all
I'll not marry at all

I'll not marry a man that's rich
To laugh at my ways and call me Bitch
And I'll not marry a man that's poor
To wear down my bones on a bare pine floor
And I'll not marry a man that's mean
To give me a baby and leave me clean

Go away from my window you ramblers uncertain
For I'll never marry Jeremiah Martin

I'll not marry who my mother chooses
Tell him Mary Eliza refuses
And I'll not marry the preacher's son
And sit at the table and gnaw on a bone
And I'll not marry up Sawney Creek
Where the mockingbird flies and never comes back

No I'll not marry at all at all
Eliza won't marry at all

Tell all the young men that when they beg
I sit on a chair and swing my leg
I'd rather hear a jay in a sweetgum tree
Than Jeremiah Martin come courting me
Go away from my window go away go away
For you won't bide till my wedding day

And I'll not marry
Never at all
I'll never marry at all.

II
Willie Rejected

One morning one morning one morning in May
When the daisy prospered on the hill
It came to curlyhead Will to go
To search the fountain of blue day.
And having gone a mile or two
He meets the daughter of the mill
And offers her a lily-white lie
For the taste of pleasuring honey.

"Oh Mary, our miller's smiling daughter,
I'll never betray you till time's end
To the wild boys' crow-black laughter,
To the hunchback gossip and her scarecrow friend."

"I'll not go with you, handy Will.
I know a maiden is betrayed
When the handy man has taken his fill
Then takes his legs on the long long road.
The maiden betrayed must turn her face
Always to look in shadow where
She sees the form of winter disgrace
Darken the Maytime lightsome air."

"I would not force my argument,"
Said Will. "The long long road is free
And wild as the cloudy firmament
And green with heartloose gaiety."

Mary turned back to her cheerful house
And said her solemn prayers to God.
She fed with crumbs her little brown mouse
And dreamed of legs on the long long road
Until it seemed her walls had blown
Away and all outdoors marched in
And cracked the roof of the flour mill down
And opened it all to the wind and rain.

III
Willie Haunted

Who is knocking at my window?
Who is mourning that pitiful mourn?

I am your truelove knocking at your window,
Sweetheart you shall never see again,
For you've unloosed the knot that bound us
And set me to wander like the windy rain.

It was the falsest turn you could ever do me,
To tell your traitor lies and say my name
In places where the cold steel knives could hear you,
In places where the hard men never go home.

You've mocked and told my name in dreadful places,
In houses where the eyes of mockers glint like water,
And I am turned upon the wandering mountain,
And I have ceased to be my mother's daughter.

Why are you knocking at my window?
Why are you mourning that pitiful mourn?

I come back lonesome in the wind to curse you
And carry your name across the wounded hill
To tell the daughters of the loving mothers
It's a poison heart in the breast of curlyhead Will.

Go, go away from my window.
Go mourn your sorrows on the shaggy mountain.

IV
Willie's Farewell to the City

And who will kiss your ruby lips
When I am gone away?

Red ladies, I take my leave of you
And reach my thin old suitcase down
And fill it up with guitar strings,
One pair of shoes not broken in,
Down Glitter Street to the Trailways station
And as far away as a weary man can.

And who will glove your hand?

It's the sight of the moon has turned my mind
Where it rides free and rolls the night
Like it rolled the hills I left behind
To learn my heart too late too late.

When I'm gone away ten thousand miles
Ten thousand miles from home

V
Not Willie's Fault

Going to get me a pistol
Just as long as I am tall

If you ask in the tavern, if you ask in the court,
They'll tell you that Willie ain't the murdering sort.
My life ain't been easy, but my life has been right,
I never had trouble sleeping at night.

I never stole nothing, I never told lies,
Till I looked too deep down in Deborah's eyes
And saw there a witch-light that spelled out my name.
Lord from that moment I ain't been the same.

A pistol
Long as I am tall

Now I never was hellbent, I want you to know,
Till I started to ramble with Cotton Eye Joe,
And I never was Wanted nor been on the run
Till I started up whiskey with Clinch River Dan.

My cards come up Aces with never a Deuce,
I stayed off the women and stayed off the juice
And went to church Sundays and bowed down my head,
And now they come tell me John Jackson is dead.

Get me a pistol
Long and mean and tall

Now if you go asking all over this land
Folks will say Willie's a sweetminded man.
Go ask my mother that lives in Scrub Holler
If Willie didn't bring her his every other dollar.

Go ask my sister that married the preacher
If Willie ain't truly a gentlehearted creature.
But don't ask the sheriff and don't ask Judge Carse,
They sentenced sweet Willie thirty years behind bars.

Going to get me a pistol
Just as long as I am tall
And shoot that witch-eye Deborah
Just to hear her weep and bawl.

VI
The Hard Pull

I never look up to see the sky
But what I think of the long highway,
The bush hook flashing and the water can,
The big mosquitoes and the trusty-man,
The sun coming down like Armageddon,
And Mary Eliza's long-ago wedding.
And it's a hard pull for poor old Willie.

There's twenty-five years stretch out before me
Of burning weather and weather stormy,
Twenty-five years of light bread and beans
And rusty water and stiff brogans,
Twenty-five years of girls on my mind
And all the free life I left behind.
Hard hard times for poor old Willie
Sweet Willie's fallen the long hard pull

Young fellows come hear me, don't pay no mind
To the faithless promise of the wind,
Watch out your whiskey and quiet your laughter
Or you'll go marry the ropemaker's daughter
And cause your mother to grieve so keen
She'll wish there was never a world of men.
Hard times hard times for poor sweet Willie.

Sometimes at night I see in dream
The green and welcome fields of home
And see my mother by her table,
Stitching a shroud with threads of cable,
And a snow comes down inside the room
And covers up her every seam.
And it's hard times for poor old Willie,
Sweet Willie's fallen the long hard pull.

VII
The Regret of Mary

Look back look back the Maytime days
Look back all the green valley

Sometimes the morning strikes my curtain
    With a light so clean and bright
I forget I married Jeremiah Martin
    One Saturday night.

And forget I've got a flintrock sorrow
    Thrust in my heart as deep
As ever my husband plowed his furrow
    Or slept his sleep.

Look back the Maytime days, look back

They tell me sweet Willie's been captured and tried,
    Sent up for thirty years.
On Bear Den Hill I hung my head
    And wept cold tears.

Yes I'm a good mother and faithful wife,
  Go tell the world I am,
But sometimes there haunts me a different life
  As in a dream.

Look back

Young girls take warning, take a warning from me,
  And follow your heart's desire.
Don't trade your chance to be songbird-free
  For a hearthplace fire.

Look back look back the Maytime days
Look back all the green valley

Ave atque Vale

Weeping, I mended the broken wing
Of Love and calmed his shuddering
And bound his wounded hand and then
I watched him fly away again.

In the Garden

The guitar's rubato quivered
And died. The woman shivered
And lifted toward the night her head.
He set his wine glass on the tray.
There was something fragile they had feared to say.
Now it was said.

I Love You

Yet you were gone six days before
I took from the bedroom closet the dress,
The blue and white one that you wore
To that dinner party that was such a mess,
And fearfully hung it on the door,
And sat before it in a chair,
Remembering what and when and where,
And touched it with a ghost's caress.

The Stories

The story of lovers torn apart by war is a thousand pages long.

The story of lovers whom money separates fills all the stiff
    ledgers of Europe.

By the light of a single candle I read the tale of lovers
    grown old together, climbing faithfully to the darkened
    landing of the stairway.

A Glorious Twilight

Susan is painting her nails
such a brilliant shade of bright
she seems to have sprouted 22 fingers

Don't need open-toed shoes, those toes
would gleam through blind galoshes
like designer Northern Lights

Be careful, I said, waving your phalanges about!
You're gonna burn the house down

And then the house began to bulge
With the light of fingernails
And lifted through the air
Through clouds where it snows and hails
And came to rest beside
The pale-by-comparison moon
And glowed on the earnest astronomer
Like a Passion Fire doubloon

Recovery of Sexual Desire After a Bad Cold

Toward morning I dreamed of the Ace of Spades reversed
And woke up giggling.
New presence in the bedroom, as if it had snowed,
And an obdurate stranger come to visit my body.

This is how it all renews itself, floating down
Mothlike on the shallow ebb of sleep,
How Easter arrives, and the hard-bitten dogwood
Flowers, and waters run clean again.

I am a new old man.
As morning sweetens the forsythia and the cats
Bristle with impudent hungers, I learn to smile.
I am a new baby.

What woman could turn from me now?
Shining like a butter knife, and the fever burned off,
My whole skin alert as radar, I can think
Of nothing at all but love and fresh coffee.

Poems of Character

A poet desires invisibility
When he attempts a faithful portraiture
Of men and women in fine-drawn miniature
That taxes to the limit his artistry.
He must observe subtly, himself unseen
By subject or by watchful audience,
Details and traits that limn his figures clean
Against the background of their circumstance.

And yet he's not like news photographers
Clicking pictures of the merely *there,*
Their images a humdrum daily fare
Like oatmeal. Rubens and his *Venus in Furs*
Is more the sort of thing I have in mind,
Or Raphael's portrait of Castiglione:
Comprehensions piercing but refined,
Delicate as flowers, luxurious as money.

The task requires such balanced sympathies
His efforts risk the peril of being bland
And spiritless as yards of Gobi sand,
With all the pungence of Velveeta cheese.
Yet if he once obtrudes himself upon
His subject and decides to step between
Viewer and canvas, all his work has gone
For naught, however skillful is his pen.

Therefore, go softly, when you set out to draw
The character of a fellow human being.
There are certain proprieties of seeing
That you must follow as if they were law.
Speak modestly, always with measured love,
And of but noble pious traits discourse,
As in this song from page 100 of
The Oxford Book of Medieval Latin Verse:

In the town of Angers there did bide
An abbot named Adam known far and wide
As a thirst wrapped up in monastic gown:
He could drink more wine than the whole damn town.

Yohoho *it's mighty fine*

To pour a glass

to the god of wine!

No hour that passed by day or night
In midnight dark at morning light
Found that he gave the cask relief:
He soaked like a sponge and shook like a leaf.

Yohoho, etc.

Incorruptible flesh he had put on
With wine spiced hot with cinnamon;
The wines he bibbed in every weather
Had turned his hide to burgundy leather.

Yohoho, etc.

Nor did he take a civilized sip
Lifting fine crystal to a dainty lip
But sozzled and guzzled from pots so capacious
They had to be made to his specifications.

Yohoho, etc.

The town of Angers should take real pride
That the abbot named Adam there did bide;
There was never his like for elbow action
They ought to make him a tourist attraction.

Yohoho
it's mighty fine
to pour a glass
to the god of wine!

—All right, I will admit this drinking song
Is not a model of proprieties,
That my preamble was an obvious tease,
And that this prologue's running rather long.
The trouble is that poems of character
Are hard to link with any sort of herb
And that the structure of my book must square
In every part—noun, adjective, and verb,

Stanza form and rhyme—with the design
Of forming a vernal *salade composée,*
A complex metaphor that should display
Fresh variety in every line,
But with an unremitting consistency
Of vision. And that, Susan, is very hard
To do—or anyhow it is for me;
And just as difficult for l'ancien Ronsard.

Fern seed renders us invisible,
Lends acuteness to our comprehension,
To empathy adds a wider dimension,
And helps us think until our minds are full.
So the folklore says, at any rate,
And must have driven wild the herbalist
Who went abroad to seek it early and late:
Because, of course, fern seed does not exist.

It is necessary to consume
The fern itself in order to acquire
Those legendary powers poets aspire
To. Marlowe's Faustus, before he met his doom,
Performed invisibly many a deed
By means of this magic. Shakespeare's *Dream*
Demonstrates the virtues of fern seed.
So here's a recipe with nutmeg cream:

Collect your ferns when in the fiddlehead
Stage of growth. Make certain that the scroll
Is snugly curled into a tight green roll
As tender as the clouds in a thunderhead,
Then snip it off no more than an inch below.
It's covered with a spiny little fuzz
You must remove. Then five minutes or so
In boiling water and lemon juice.

Meanwhile, whip one cup of heavy cream
With a quarter teaspoonful of salt till nearly
Thick and add the nutmeg, but go fairly
Light. A teaspoon and a half will seem
Enough for normal palates. You mustn't lose
The woodsy flavor of your April ferns.
Serve them decorated with cashews
And wash them down with honey-gold Sauternes.

Transmogrification of the Diva

May she lie sleeping still
While the disarranged powders dust the frayed
Pink crinkled ribbons adrift on mother-of-pearl.
The castrato cat at bedfoot dozes, his eyes
Plump-shut with drowse. She will not restlessly stir,
    Half-open hands at peace.

    Keep the squabbles of tenors
Far now from her whole rest; let the curtain rise
Over the pit, floodlight knifing above
The horns and varnished oboes; let Maestro
Carve the unfathomable score, while she
    In-breathes the musk of time.

    Let the audience yet crave
Her ghost-glimmer in the second act:
That sweet note the young soprano cannot form.
Let it then transpire: pure clean shaft
Of music open her breast to the trompe l'oeil skies
    Where the gilt swans stream.

Dipperful

"Help yourself to a drink, it's toted fresh."

My hand rose in the water to meet my hand
And in its shadow his sweet spring appeared.
Mica-grains swarmed out of the hill-womb,
A crawfish trailed a funnel of yellow sand.
I drank the hill. A scatter of sand-motes sparkled
When I launched the gourd's blind belly back in the bucket,
And on my tongue the green hill sprouted ferns.

Went back to jaw and ravel the afternoon
With the old man on his porch that shaded his hounds
Beneath, warm spotted lumps of doze and quiver.
I sat down easy to watch at ease the cornfield
Across the creek get tall.

              "Been walking far?"

"Not half as far," I said, "as my feet would say."
He nodded and thumbed a twisted cigarette shut.
"Used to," he said, "I'd wear the daylight out,
I'd trudge till my cartridges was gone. I shot
To death I swear to God all of the pokeweed
In Johnson's pasture. That would keep me going.
A boy'll walk to the end of the world, not thinking."

"Sure. But when you had to walk to work—"

"—They couldn't inch me along with a twelve-pound sledge.
But if we didn't have the triflingness
To think back on, nobody would come this far."

"How far?"

           "Eighty years this coming December."
He spat and watched it roll up in the dust,
Leaned back, and thought the thoughts an old man thinks.
I felt myself slide off the edge of his mind.
Dreaming, he spoke. "What hinders my sleep most
Is my daddy's boots. Here they come a-sailing

At me when I shut my eyes, bobbing
Off the floor by his bedside, great things
That felt as hard as iron when I was a youngun.
The way he kept them candled, rubbing and rubbing
At night to keep the water out, the way
The upper hooks would shine like a black cat's eyes.
I'd ponder on them, how strong I'd have to be
When I got growed to march my boots along.
Can't I just hear him puffing whenever he'd bend
Over to lace them to the top? His hair
Flopped down on his face. He'd straighten up
And stare at nothing, the day that was coming ahead.

"I recall one time I reached my hand in there.
Jerked it out again, for that surprised me,
How hot his boots got, hot as fresh fire coals.
All day long the old man's walking in fire,
I thought, and thought I didn't want
To olden and walk in fire the way he did.
And I don't know I did, the way he did.
I never got married, you see, never had
To grub for other people. I worked enough
To keep myself a peaceful sufficiency.
The world ain't all that lonesome for more MacReadies.
Now I'm so busted down there ain't much left,
But not a burden to some old muley woman."

He spat again and a swoon of flies unsettled,
Then settled back. The early afternoon
Began to climb the fields. "I've talked too much,"
He said. "I wish I didn't talk so much."
When he said that, the silence had its say.

Remodeling the Hermit's Cabin

an epilogue to the Constitution of the United States

Not what we expected. And dark in there,
The one little window not a proper window,
But a choppy off-square page of cloud and treetop
That let a grayness in. No pinup girls
Leggy in froth panties, but recipes
On the walls, heavy crayons of eagles,
Torn-out leaves of Bibles, pictures of flowers.
"This old feller was a different kind of lonesome,"
Reade said. We didn't understand. The bed
Was rusty, stoic, narrow. The floor was bare.

We found his handiwork. A carved and sanded
Walking stick with a twice-twined rattlesnake
Leaned in the corner. Ferrule and knob smeared silverish,
The snake was blotched unlikely black and orange.
Reade hefted it for balance. "I've seen worse,"
He said. "This old-time whittling, you always wonder
Where they got the hours. I bet I've started
A dozen, and never finished one I'd carry."

In a corner shelf we found his Little People,
Whittled men and women and children hand-sized,
Naked or dressed in closely twisted cornshuck,
Disposed in attitudes forlorn and studied,
Each inhabiting a single space
That set it well apart from all the others,
Even in the narrow shelf. "His folks,"
Reade said, "how he remembers the way it was.
You see they didn't get along too good,
But what the story is would be a puzzle.

This one here is him." The only doll
He didn't give a face, an oval of soft
White pine blank as a thumbnail, a spindly figure
Turned toward the ragged chinked log wall, unclothed,
And set apart from the scene the other dolls

Absorbed themselves in, deaf or contemptuous
Of passions fierce for all their littleness,
Fiercer perhaps because of littleness—
A figure the world had cut no features on,
Musing the figureless wall that was his mirror.

We swept them all into a cardboard box.

Outside we gathered our courage. "That Florida buyer
Wants us to raise the roof," Reade said, "and lower
The floor. Might be we'll do the roof okay,
Just loosen the nails and shim it up with blocks
Wedged in under the joists. But would you look
At them foundation beams? That main one there
Must be two-and-a-half foot square, and dug in
Solid where it's set two hundred years."

"Whose cabin was it before the hermit came?"

"Old hunting lodge from maybe nineteen hundred.
Before that I don't know—Daniel Boone's,
I reckon. Don't see logs like this no more."
He measured it with his tape. "What'd I tell you?
Thirty inches, and lodged into the hill
Since the flood of Noah."

                              "Well, what'll we do?"

"Rassle it," he said, "unless you've got
A better notion."

                    We wrestled it. And broke
The handle of a twelve-pound sledge, and bent
His faithful old black crowbar into a U.
We stopped for a cup of water from the S-
shaped runlet below the spring. "Takes a grade-A
Fool to start this ruinous job," Reade said.
"They could've paid us to cut a window or two
And left it like it was. There ain't no way
To get the foundation stout like it used to be."

"What do you guess it cost to build this cabin?"

"Twenty-eight dollars, twelve and one-half cents,
In pure cash money. Then you've got your labor,
And the brains it took to think the construction out,
And whatever it's worth to stand out independent
And be thought wild or crazy or just plain dumb."

"It looks kind of sad and busted, what we've done,"
I said.
              "That Florida feller will tack up plastic,"
He said, "and put him in an ice machine,
And have a radar carport and a poodle
He's trained to count his money. These modern days
We're all a bunch of cowbirds, you know that?"

The Presences at Sunset

(untitled etching by Mary Anne Sloan)

"Halfstep by palsied halfstep she has come
As if compelled by a remembered dream."

"A shawl about her shoulders, a gnarly stick
To search the path that wends so rough and black."

"The years have settled on her like the silence
Of a shuttered house that once knew violence."

"She rarely lifts her head. The setting sun
Is thin and strange on the scarred horizon."

"Now she arrives, a weary penurious widow,
Where shadow reigns, where all light is shadow."

"A stand of alders guards the deep still pool.
No stars, no moon. The lengthened hour grows cool."

"Why does she come here? This water like dull slate
Can hold no image of a human fate."

"She comes because a half-lost memory
Whispers to her like a distant sea."

The Widow

And then unhappiness enfolded her
Like a sleeping rose, and she dropped through
The billows of its perfume as if rising
Through an evening mist to greet a star.
Alone inside this flower she felt no fear,
Such sharp authority her sorrow held.
Her Age of Reason opened like a Sahara.

The Voices

The whisper that was the shadow of surmise,
The percales that were the moon's cool bandages,
The murmurs of the raindrop yesterdays
Descending past the streaming dormer windows,
The hours that were apartments where it snows
And nothing lives though nothing ever dies
Except the echoes and the promises
And afternoons of shrouded silences:

More than the death she fears these memories
The widow fears because there are no faces
In them, no hands, no blood-warm presences
To summon back the common intimacies
That must have been her life, the life that voices
Disquieten now with ceaseless susuruss.

The Reader

for Helene Nicholls

Beside the floor lamp that has companioned her
For decades, in her Boston rocking chair,
Her body asks a painful question of the books.
Her fingers are so smooth and white
They reflect the pages; a light
The color of cool linen bathes her hands.
The books read into her long through the night.

There is a book that opens her like a fan: and so
She sees herself, her life, in delicate painted scenes
Displayed between the ivory ribs that may close up
The way she claps the book shut when she's through
The story that has no end but cannot longer go.
It doesn't matter what the story means;
Better if it has no meaning—or just enough
For her to say the sentence that she likes to say:
Why do these strange folks do the way they do?

And yet they comfort her, being all
That she could never be nor wish to be;
They bring the world—or some outlook of its soul—
Into her small apartment that is cozy
As the huddling place of an animal
No one is yet aware of, living in
A secret corner of a secret continent,
An animal that watches, wonders, while the moon
Rides eastward and the sun comes up again
Over a forest deep as an ocean and as green.

An Old Mountain Woman Reading the Book of Job

The veiny wrist, the knobby finger joints,
The scar-creased palm, the thumb she lifts to wet
And lift the corner of the memoried page,
Turning once more through Job's bewilderment:
What histories are written into her hand . . .

Aforetime she was as a tabret, but now
They change the night to day, the light is short,
The world delivered to ungodly shadow.
The darkness of her hand darkens the page.
She straightens her bifocals in which the words,
Reflected, jitter, then come to rest like moths.
It is November. The woodstove shifts its log
And grumbles. The night is longer than her fire.

She moves her lips to read but does not speak.
What is there to answer to the terrible words,
To these sharp final words that engrave the fate
Of an old man hammered to bronze. She sees the man
As if he stood before her, thrown by the storm
Of time to be her husband, her dead husband.
She knows the man as man, his house and fields
Up Jarvis Creek going down in sawbriar,
The doctor bills chewing the farm like locusts.
Bleak Job scourged ceaseless in the starless night,
Her husband whom lean ravishment made holy:
The whirlwind-savage hand of God forecloses
The mortgage; the fields are auctioned clod by clod,
The skies are auctioned cloud by pallid cloud.

The Book of Job draws all its shadow over
Her thumbed-limp Bible. Saint Paul does not escape,
Jesus Himself does not shine clear of Job,
The darkness of that blindly punished lament.
Shall any teach God knowledge? —But if He knows,
And still permits . . .

                              There is a weeping madness
In thoughts she tries so tiredly to push away.
Her trust lies down in dirt like a fractured tower.

Everything shall be restored, the Book
Tells her. But why should it be taken away?
Or given at the start? Her husband Charles,
The man she knows as Job, mild unto death,
She doubts shall be restored. The Book of Job
Distills to salt in the tear that seals her eye.

Let her then go out on Ember Mountain,
And cry out in his stead and say those words
She shall imagine for him, picturing
Herself there in the dark, in pitiless wind,
Raising her old fist to dare the lightning
And gates of wrath, herself alone in wind,
Saying the words that God's wind lacerates.
Let it be her stricken, blasted, shriveled
Like a candlewick and not the man
Her husband, whom the Lord like a hunting lion
Has carried off, her Job who suffered silence
As he went down never to rise again.

That silence does not yield. Her vision tears;
She never shall curse God, she never shall
Climb Ember Mountain again, nor ever weep.

But now she feels a throb in this old house
In which she sits alone, nursing her fire,
Her fear. A tremor as of someone walking
Another room, the kitchen or cold bedroom.
Someone unfamiliar is walking there,
Someone no kin to her, maybe no friend,
Who comes to bring her tidings the dead have risen
And all the wholeness of the earth restored.
She holds her breath; the phantom goes away.

She shuts the book of Job. She will not suffer
A God Who suffers the suffering of man,
Who sends the fatherless their broken arms,
Who sends away the widows empty of faith.
Tonight's no night for the heartless bedside prayer.

My Grandmother Washes Her Feet

I see her still, unsteadily riding the edge
Of the clawfoot tub, mumbling to her feet,
Musing bloodrust water about her ankles.
Cotton skirt pulled up, displaying bony,
Bruised, and patchy calves that would make you weep.

Rinds of her soles had darkened, breadcrust-colored—
Not yellow now—like the tough outer belly
Of a snake. In fourteen hours the most refreshment
She'd given herself was dabbling her feet in the water.

"You mightn't have liked John Giles. Everyone knew
He was a mean one, galloping whiskey and women
All night. Tried to testify dead drunk
In church one time. That was a ruckus. Later
Came back a War Hero, and all the young men
Took to doing the things he did. And failed.
Finally one of his women's men shot him."

"What for?"

       "Stealing milk through fences . . . That part
Of Family nobody wants to speak of.
They'd rather talk about strong men, brick houses,
Money. Maybe you ought to know, teach you
Something."

       "What *do* they talk about?"

          "Generals,
And the damn old Civil War, and marriages.
Things you brag about in the front of Bibles.
You'd think there was arms and legs of Family
On every battlefield from Chickamauga
To Atlanta."

       "That's not the way it is?"

"Don't matter how it is. No proper way
To talk, is all. It was nothing they ever did.
And plenty they never talk about . . . John Giles!"

Her cracked toes thumped the dingy tub wall, spreading
Shocklets. Amber toenails curled like shavings.
She twisted the worn knob to pour in coolness
I felt suffuse her body like a whiskey.

"Bubba Martin, he was another, and no
Kind of man. Jackleg preacher with the brains
Of a toad. Read the Bible sideways crazy
Till it drove him crazy, marking craziness
On doorsills, windows, sides of Luther's barn.
He killed hisself at last with a twelve-gauge shotgun.
No gratitude for Luther putting him up
For twenty years. Shot so's to fall down the well."

"I never heard."

                    "They never mention him.
And not Aunt Annie, that everybody called
Paregoric Annie, that roamed the highways
Thumbing cars and begging change to keep
Even with her craving. She claimed to save up
To buy a glass eye. It finally shamed her sisters
Enough, they went together and got her one.
That didn't stop her. She toted it around
In a velvet-lined case, asking strangers
Please to drop it in the socket for her.
They had her put away. And that was that.
There's places Family ties just won't stretch to."

Born then in my mind a race of beings
Unknown and monstrous. I named them Shadow-Cousins,
A linked long dark line of them,
Peering from mirrors and chortling in closets, eager
To manifest themselves inside myself.
Like discovering a father's cancer.
I wanted to search my body for telltale spots.

"Sounds like a bunch of cow thieves."

                              "Those too, I reckon,
But they're forgotten or covered over so well
Not even I can make them out. Gets foggy

When folks decide they're growing respectable.
First thing you know, you'll have a Family Tree."

(I pictured a scraggy wind-stunted horse-apple.)

She raised her face. The moons of the naked bulb
Flared in her glasses, painting out her eyes.
In dirty water light bobbed like round soap.
A countenance matter-of-fact, age-engraved,
Mulling in peaceful wonder petty annals
Of embarrassment. Gray but edged with brown
Like an old photograph, her hair shone yellow.
A tiredness mantled her fine energy.
She shifted, sluicing water under instep.

"O what's the use," she said. "Water seeks
Its level. If your daddy thinks that teaching school
In a stiff white shirt makes him a likelier man,
What's there to blame? Leastways, he won't smother
Of mule-farts or have to starve for a pinch of rainfall.
Nothing new gets started without the old's
Plowed under, or halfway under. We sprouted from dirt,
Though, and it's with you, and dirt you'll never forget."

"No Mam."

                    "Don't you say me No Mam yet.
Wait till you get your own chance to deny it."

Once she giggled, a sound like stroking muslin.

"You're bookish. I can see you easy a lawyer
Or a county clerk in a big white suit and tie,
Feeding the preacher and bribing the judge and sheriff.
Second-generation-respectable
Don't come to any better destiny.
But it's dirt you rose from, dirt you'll bury in.
Just about the time you'll think your blood

Is clean, here comes dirt in a natural shape
You never dreamed. It'll rise up saying, Fred,
Where's that mule you're supposed to march behind?
Where's your overalls and roll-your-owns?
Where's your Blue Tick hounds and Domineckers?
Not all the money there is can wash true-poor rich.
Fatback just won't change to artichokes."

"What's artichokes?"

                              "Pray Jesus you'll never know.
For if you do it'll be a sign you've grown
Away from what you are, can fly to flinders
Like a touch-me-not . . . I may have errored
When I said *true-poor.* It ain't never the same
As dirt-poor. When you got true dirt you got
Everything you need . . . And don't you say me
Yes Mam again. You just wait."

                              She leaned
And pulled the plug. The water circled gagging
To an eye and poured in the hole like a rat.
I thought that maybe their spirits had gathered there,
All my Shadow-Cousins clouding the water,
And now they ran to earth and would cloud the earth.
Effigies of soil, I could seek them out
By clasping soil, forcing warm rude fingers
Into ancestral jelly my father wouldn't plow.
I strained to follow them, and never did.
I never had the grit to stir those guts.
I never had the guts to stir that earth.

Overheard in the Tea Room

"Marianne, my dear,
I'll say this for Ruth:
Though she never tells the truth
Her lies are quite sincere."

Third Base Coach

He commands as mysteriously
as the ghost of Hamlet's father.

Shuffles & tugs & yawns & spits.
Like a steeplejack he itches weirdly and continually.

Dances on his grave plot
as if the secrets in his head were Walkman music.

Writes runes with his toe.
The fouls go by him like tracer bullets.

Like an Aeschylean tragedy he's static,
Baffling, boring, but.
                          Urgent with import.

Fast Ball

for Winthrop Watson

The grass raw and electric
as the cat's whiskers.

3 and 2.

At second the runner loiters,
nervous as the corner junkie
edgy for a connection.

Hunched like a cat, the batter:
his prehensile bat
he curls and uncurls.

The pitcher hitches & hitches.

At last the hitcher pitches.

"It gets about the size," Ty Cobb said,
"of a watermelon seed.
It hisses as it passes."

The outfielders tumble like kittens
back to the benches.
Baseball's a game of light-speeds.
And inches.

Junk Ball

By the time it gets to the plate
the ump has grown a beard.

Like trying to hit Wednesday with a bb gun.
On Sunday.

Or it swerves like a Chippendale leg
or flutters like a film unsprocketed
or plunges like the starlet's neckline
or comes in slower than a poker-debt payoff.

Not even Mussolini
could make the sonofabitch arrive on time.

Spitballer

A poet because his hand
goes first to his heart and then to his head.

The catcher receives the pitch
the way a blotter takes an ink spill.

The hitter makes much show
of wringing out his bat.

On the mound he grins
with all his teeth at once
when the umpire inspects the ball
suddenly dry as alum.

He draws a juicy salary bonus
because when he pitches he waters the lawn.

Strike Zone

for Joe Nicholls

Like the Presidency its size
depends upon the man.

The pitcher whittles at the casement,
trying not to bust the paneless window.

The batter peers into it like a peeping tom.
Is he excited by what he sees?

The limits get stricter
as they get less visible.

Throwing at yards and yards of Willie McCovey,
a foot or so
of Luis Aparicio,
the pitcher tries not to go bats.

Umpire knows a thing or two,
but gives no sign.

Ball 3.

Dr. Bones

Dismissed for my hands-on care
Of the duchess and her vapors,
Shipped over with a thievish packet
Of hymn-singing lepers,

I arrived these shores hungry.
Tacked my shingle up:
The Doctor Is Always In.
Prescribes Dope.

During the Little War
I switched sides twice,
Stitching the wanted and unwanted,
The famous and infamous.

As chief field surgeon
To turncoat General Hood,
I steeped to my gluteals
In cold blood.

Nurse Figleaf agreed to call.
We drank the bottle off.
When Dr. Horney died she came
To my staff.

I snipped the querulous wealthy
Of the fleecy nation.
No poodle-petting matron
Escaped examination.

They found me ready and willing
When the Big War started;
I began to chip and chop
Wholehearted.

But was forced to tell my patients,
"This may cause a little pain."
No soldier under my knife
Had to soldier again.

And then the war was over
And things died down a bit.
Now I loaf and fiddle and snooze,
Running to fat.

In the lab I dust disused retorts;
There's nothing much to do.
Still I keep trying and trying to think of something
New.

Tiger in the Field of Flame Grass

Velvet bars of darkness interslash,
Crossing, recrossing in silken moiré.
The marbled head with calm intensity
Of concentration need not turn to see
When a blackbird bursts in a startled flash
From its shadow-nest into obvious day.

He has thought and thought until now he slides
Thoughtless through the head-tall flame grass.
He is as omnipresent and as noiseless
As the thoughts he thinks no more, and as he hides
He conceals nothing, being in this place
But blades of light amid the other blades.

The way is open before him. His mastery
Of time is absolute; he is in time,
Just as in light, part of the saffron flame
Of it, burning forward steadily
Toward the unalterable purpose of the game.

Soon he will come to where the grass grows thin.
The waterhole beyond with its blue-clay muck
Will crowd with weary prey. His ears flat back,
He'll crouch and watch and wait, intent upon
The populist candidate in his limousine.

Latencies

First point of light and then another and another: the stars
come out, bright dredge-net lifting from darkness
those many heroes we read the mind with.
This is the notion of *latency* I partly drew from books.

Suppose there is no present time, only the latent past now manifest.
A trout rising to the noon river surface reinstates the dawn,
whiff of it here where I tie on the Adams. The trout is silent;
the hour is a latent prayer I am afraid to say aloud.

The woman stands by the window, strikes a posture
that suddenly recalls to me a decade of mazy dreams.
The window is a latent religion. Thrust open,
what new powers, new immanence, pour in upon us.

Or consider my young friend fishing the river.
Now he has gone to be a soldier, has become
a latent garden of American Beauty roses
that only the enemy shrapnel can make scarlet.

Some of It

Everybody got shot
They laid down in flags or came back in giblets
I sniveled after girls I couldn't get it up for
And fumbled the bottles over the chipped formica
And dreamed of debriefings and the wrong LZ coordinates

Roberto and Bill came by the ward to cheer me
But all I remember are teeth snapping like breech bolts
At last I told Dr. Will and his ugly nurse to shove it
And marched back to The Zulu Lounge to heal myself
After that for a year nothing comes clean to my head

I got some shit from a full disability hero
Who told me he'd killed a girl in Can Tho or Kansas
Or was it me that killed her, he had to ask
Detective Sgt. Rico told me to leave New Jersey
But slipped me a bottle of Rocket at the Trailways station

My bowels were busted, my molars glowed with pain
In the snow by the firebarrel I watched my footprints wander
I heard an old man bleeding under the trestle
And went to have a look and sure enough
I polished off the pint the corpse was deserting

I usually make believe I survived but now
When I dig my left hand through the mud of this blue ditch
I'm sure I feel something pumping that doesn't stop
It must be the mighty big whiskey heart of the world
The hot whiskey heart that makes the dying sociable

Score

An ordinary street scene anywhere—
Or in New Haven, as it happens to be—
With twilight edging in, the air
Tinged orange, the pimps already
Checking out the traffic, strutting as the sun
Goes down and down,
Falling like a liquid stone
Just as the dark and all its knives come on.

The midnight of the needle
And the nickel. The fairway suburbs send
Their shaken daughters out to wheedle
The ominous stranger and habitual friend.
She delivers her snowy intelligence;
Her emptied eyes declare
A whole Manhattan of indifference,
A whole Miami of despair.

Meanwhile

A man must get ahead in the world.
He must kiss, in prescribed and ancient order,
the lipworn arses of his goldplate ministry
superiors. It is a form of prayer,

he feels. Because the man who gets ahead
must show his piety, must hang the costly drapes
of burgundy velvet in the sitting room . . .
The house plunges its spear into his side.

At midnight in the paneled library he pours
a brandy and tries to think about his life.
He ponders instead his career, which gleams
like a samovar. Now he is tired, dull pain

beneath his heart, he must begin
a sensible diet tomorrow. Meanwhile, picquet.
Meanwhile, gossip and roast veal. Meanwhile,
meanwhile. Death pays an informal call

and they talk for an hour, but the chat is banal.
He explains that he is merely ordinary,
a man of middle rank, he had not expected
a visitor so distinguished. The torture

is that it never felt like torture, the horror
is that it was always ordinary always.
A man must get ahead in the world,
the world that breaks its first and only promise.

Teller

The money appears as jittery fireflies
Her black screen has netted. They suspend
A moment within their small abyss;
They tell their little story and go away.
Her computer circumspectly peeps, displays
New constellations of number without end,
Mint-green and cool and dry,
As fleeting and irrevocable as a kiss.

What an ardent gossip it is, this sleek machine!
Nothing but rumors of money the livelong day.
It tells her everything but where the money is,
Or if it really exists. Probably
It doesn't exist. It's only Business,
Something you have to take on faith to mean
Something: a ghost, like PERKINS, P T, whose name
Appears before her in letters of unnatural flame.

And isn't this the truth no one is telling?
The people don't exist, nor even the money.
Nothing is out there but the boxes trilling
To one another, and their solitary tenders who
Provide the numbers and then wipe them away.
It must be true that numbers alone
Exist, and everything else is an observant machine
That registers digits the Number God has sown
Upon the limitless midnight and the measureless day.

The Bible of the Unlucky Sailor

The sea blots Genesis, sea salt ruins
to blood the red words of Jesus who plodded—
remember, Kelly?—across the waves. Kelly's
Bible, one of his brother's hand-me-downs,
seesaws tumbling above his head, prodded
by determined currents. Kelly descends until he's
at the bottom of the world, where suns
don't dart their light to, where a man unmans.

The book of holy code is a better swimmer,
sidling from wave to wave like a jellyfish,
disgorging its text as June disgorges summer
into an ocean of time, the Word's sweet Flesh
transforming once again in heavy seas,
becoming a sea-thing strange beyond surmise.

Poems of Fantasy

O Cloud-capp'd Towers and gorgeous Palaces!
O Mermaids, Goblins, Unicorns, and Fairies!
O Brownies that inhabit homes and dairies!
O Triton, Hippogriff, and Giantess!
O figures of sumptuous Imagining,
Come lend my stanzas mist and mystery,
Climb upon my tropes and wildly sing
Of golden legend, fabled history!

Come, succubus and jeweled hetaera
Of mage by puissant spell brought forth from ages
Lost in dust-heaped time! Come, Seven Sages!
Merlin, come! Come, Et Cetera!
We enter now the realm of fantasy,
Of whimsy, speculation, tale and dream,
The province that belongs to poetry
Which sees things as they are *and* as they seem.

Of course, it's not to everybody's taste,
This cotton-candy universe of figures
That some find substanceless as fumes of liquors
Swarming the brains of wretches who write in haste
Anything to stir an untidy mind.
There is no literature that can please all,
And disbelievers are not hard to find.
For example, here's my friend Don Hall:

BALLADE OF THE SKEPTIC DONALD HALL

"I have no hankering to start a quarrel;
It's just that I prefer the genuine,
The world with its froggy warts, and not some floral
Arrangement prettifying with cute design
The homely truths that poets must see plain
And take excruciating pains to tell.
The vein of Fact is the only vein to mine.
I hate bloody Tolkien!" said Donald Hall.

"Bill Stafford draining his a.m. sump is moral;
Your whorehouse Baudelaire I would consign
To oblivion, his mistresses with coral
Lips and practices I can't condone.
If only the Frenchman had possessed but one
Jersey cow to milk and played baseball,
He might have written something really fine.
I hate exoticism!" said Donald Hall.

"Poets should celebrate the fresh auroral
Virtues of New England and draw a line
Straightedge between the real and the irreal,
And when they don't their failure is condign.
I wish I had authority to assign
A Poland China to poets one and all—
It's soon enough they'd learn to buckle down
And eschew all fantasy," said Donald Hall.

"So, Fred, the next time you take up your pen
To answer what you think is the Muses' call,
Include a hog or two. Show some spine!
I hate that faërie crap," said Donald Hall.

—Well, there go Chaucer, Shakespeare, Spenser out
The window, not to mention poor John Keats.
I will admit a steady diet of sweets
Is not a wise one and maybe causes gout.
Consider, though, what literature would be
If only Emile Zola and George Crabbe
Held frosty sway and no hyperbole
Ever brightened landscapes of olive drab.

We might as well read government reports,
Stock market listings, actuarial
Pie-charts, immigration figures, and all
The thrilling records of the traffic courts.
Someone said of American poetry
That like the shark it must contain a shoe.
But why must it include the factory,
The trucks, the warehouse, and the sales tax too?

We mustn't give the bureaucrats control
Of that reality poems portray,
For if the number-crunchers have their way
They'll add our reading to the welfare roll.
It's time to start a dreamer's revolution;
All we fantasists will go on strike
And let the statisticians supply the nation
With the kind of vision they may think they'd like.

Meanwhile I'll withdraw to cool Arcadia
Replete with nymphs and oreads and fauns,
With stately oaks and marguerita'd lawns,
And girls with names like Topaz, Star, and Nadia.
And there I'll read my much-maligned Baudelaire
And try to figure out what's going on
In all those poems opulent and rare,
Like his symbolic sonnet "Les Cochons":

When they have reached a wise maturity
The austere philosopher and fervent lover
Adore the hog, for in him they discover
A being like themselves: sedentary,

Enamored of knowledge and of luxury,
Who seeks out corners where frightful shadows hover,
Who never to plow and harness will give over,
Humbling his pride to abject slavery.

His majesty, while he is sleeping, shows
Itself like a great sphinx in lone repose;
He sleeps as if his dreaming had no end;

With magic sparks his tenderloin glows
And, cloudily, in his prophetic eyes
Golden motes twinkle like grains of sand.

All writing needn't tour main-traveled roads;
Some of it should have the nerve to pierce
That naturalism defined by Ambrose Bierce:

"Reality as she is viewed by toads."
Strike through the mask! courageous Melville said,
Echoing thoughts of Edgar Allan Poe;
"Our bones are clothed in a new flesh and blood . . .
O tumults and visions!" wrote wild Rimbaud.

So let our salad employ some herbs conducive
To midnights of phantasmagoria,
To trance and reverie, euphoria
And nightmare, specters weeping and elusive.
Not opium or its derivatives
That cause the nation so much bloody grief,
But that forgotten mysterious plant that gives
Dreams of the planet Xiccarph with its leaf:

Pantagruelion, which is described
In confusing fashion in the Voynich Manuscript
Lately discovered in a disused crypt
By that same antiquarian who robbed
Choice pages of the *Necronomicon*
From the Miskatonic Library,
Hoping to trace the bloodlines one by one
In his unhappy genealogy.

And there are rumors too of other plants
That, imbibed by the rules of the old grimoire,
Liber Ivonis, transport the spirit far;
The *Book of Dzyan* offers helpful hints
And some find clues in *Codex Dagonensis.*
Other herbs are common, close to home—
Take care, though, with your *Urtica garrettensis,*
And Spreading Gioia has been known to roam.

Consult the *Hortus Parvus* of Stuart Wright
For sound advice on how to dig up roots
For preservation, how to protect new shoots
From frost and the skillful predators of night,
How to mingle drugs with Watney's ale
So that their presence cannot be detected
And the hapless victim cannot help but swill
Till all his powers of reason are infected.
But for the dedicated visionary
Such artificial aids are little use;
He has such sweet confidence in his Muse

That strong narcotics are not necessary.
So—onward now to legend, story, myth,
To Phantom Riders and Supernal Flowers,
To the elder fables that disclose such pith,
To the fairy tales that spell us bound for hours.

The Sea Text

"I'll drown my book."

The gold foil leaves waver in the current,
The sea enfolds a magic it never envied:
Secret runes, strange names, whispered spells
That cause a foreknown future to be born.
Prospero has flung his book into the water
To watch it flutter down the azure tides.

Now the sea begins to change.
This musty science, gloomy and precise,
Begins to speak its language
That knows long grief and fear and every human ache.

The sea has tasted forbidden knowledge now,
But has not lost its wild and various elegance
Where it shapes its grottoes and carves the limestone coast
Into labyrinths as involved as longing,
Elaborate as the dance
Of the stars and ceremonious moon.
The waves lap the promontory embossed with glyphs;
The sea begins to evolve new sorcerers.

Slow Harbor

The seas draw the autumn over them.
The long night heaps such wealth of stars
That lovers in the harbor town
Snuff out their lamps, take in the fretwork sky
As if entering again a childhood.

They raise their faces toward Polaris.
Cathedral of starlight
Settles upon the town like a butterfly,
Silent and tensible, unfolding its brilliant
Symmetries.   That is how it is:

Star-cathedral that slides upon the town,
As lovers slide upon one another,
Cheek and thigh and shoulder almost
Touchless.

          The onset they cannot recognize
Of winter, the early light like snow.

Visitation

The sea's blue smokes abduct the capsized town;
the visions of drowned sailors overtake
the harbor and its sullen wares. *Mother,*
I thought of you when the hull stove in, and then
the planet revolved upon my head like a moon
of pensive waters.
                Thin rainbow oil-slick
ribbons the current that the roar and slather
of storms confuse. The silent men spin down.

I feel like somebody has shipwrecked for me.
Who in the wind is calling to the sleepers?
The dark town's dreaming whitens over the sea;
the lonesome streets shine wet in the last long hours
before the sun climbs out of the hazy blue
heartless morning. *Somebody, shipwrecked for me.*

The Rose and Afterward

The rose that bruised the world was not all substance.
The spirit in it changed the spirits that it touched;
The substance of it drew each spirit to its spirit.
There was a mystery in it like a woman
With a woman's darkness and her daylight hands.

First like a cloud and then like risen mists
The rose's presence mantled sky and sea.
It was a continent of perfume, rifting, furrowing
To archipelagos and thin peninsulas.
Every object that it calmed became its subject.

The nations that it tinted lost all admiration
For intellectual things. The senses
Extended their domain until the open sea
Became a green caress and the separate stars
Were tones that sounded bell-like in their burning towers.

And then there was no knowledge of what the world
Had ever been besides the thing it was,
Whatever that might be: the history of desire
Had found its red fulfillment, the longing
That made us animal at last had made us human.

Scarecrow Colloquy

What ho, Ragwisp, how fares my Sentinel of the Stars?
Have you yet fixed for good the thrust of history?
I find you in the field as entranced as St. Jerome.

I am glad, friend, of your company.
The man who nailed me up, left me to challenge
The courage of the crow, does he still thrive?
Or has this age of snow buried him beneath?

I know him of old, high Hayhead. What would you of him?
That he unfold the motive of your wry construction?
He being who he is can never say.

The farmer he is who maintains the straggling fenceline.
He studies a-nights, the gleam of his window gives
A point to my musing. Let him come riddle me
From his big book the question and solution.

He knows you not, I tell you. He has forgotten.
The weeds and nettles of his field, his goats
And cattle, are all the business of his mind.

But does he remember me ever?
When frost has stiffened my eaten coat, I seem to see him
Rocking by the fire with his dozing meerschaum
And thinking of his friend in God, the Scarecrow.

The toil of his flesh he knows, and when
The fields are silent and his children asleep
He ponders a matter you will not wish to hear.

This autumn I have warded off the blackbird;
I have stood a steady watch while the stars went down;
I tallied the moons coasting over the stubble.
I have kept faithful till the seasons scattered.

O keep the faith, Chaffstaff, by any means.
This disaster they call a world might find a pivot
If you but stand outlined within the sunrise.

I have spoken in the field till my voice became an owl.
I have viewed the horizon till I lost my buttons.
The mouse heard my thoughts and gnawed my flesh of grass.
And still I stand here, guarding the bones of Adam.

Observers

after Einstein's *Relativity*

1

To time are added the three diversions of space:
these are the coordinates that allow us to say
Let us suppose

Let us suppose
an observer observing within this system:
To him all things are systematic

Never can he know that he supposes merely:
the wherefore of his motion
he thinks he knows without supposing

2

Yet all the consistent systems lie to one another:
the observers in their hurtling coordinates
are bound by agreement never to agree:

Because they cannot measure their respective measures:
the yardsticks shrink like accordions
the clocks contract toward yesterday

as the systems approach the friendly confines
of the speed of light, as the snail-shaped gravities
curl up in pain:

3

The separate systems veer together and apart:
the graffiti that their motions trace on space
we read as time:

It is not absolute:
the observers in their various systems
enjoy separate times and variously:

They are at rest with respect to nothing:
nothing in respect to anything is at rest:
Let us suppose nothing at rest we need ever to respect:

4

It is anyhow a universe,
the first in the history of this century,
a century clenched like mass approaching *c*:

An era when anomalies flower into laws,
the laws give rise to vivid anomalies:
a time of arbitrary starlight

which is drifting toward the place where Mozart
goes unheard forever, which is punctuated by
the blackened matchstem that was Nagasaki

(Prologue)

Beyond all borders the armies guard or plunder,
beyond the seven seas and the starry world-rim,
beyond the Glass Mountain and the Tyger Savannah,
lives a ruddy grandmama
who wears an apron with forty-seven pockets,
and in the dozenth pocket of this tattered old garment,

my story takes place.

In this country called Fernland where the grandmother lives
stands a stately oak with ninety-nine limbs,
and on each limb strut ninety-nine ravens black as trivets,
and if you do not believe the story I am going to tell,
if you do not credit every word and syllable,
the ravens will stop their prattle and fly down
to peck your eyes out:

peck   peck   peckpeck.

The Transformations: A Fairy Tale

NIGHTCAP

Two merry old scutters, the Impresario
Of Moons and the portly Maestro of Carouses
Were on the town. Hi-ho the derry-o,
The roofs were rakish on all the moonlit houses.

They lurched together like boats at anchor there
At the studded door while fuddling with the keyhole.
They were blind with jollity and sang many an air
Ringing and spiritous and quaintly medieval.

Burst into the hall like comets and flung down by
The roaring fire and roared for their tankards, they did,
And drank as deep as Occam's philosophy
From the silver tankards with satyrs and nymphs enchasèd.

They toasted the bards and declaimed their ancient verses
And drank anew as deep as eastern oceans
And saluted God Who in His grace immerses
The drunk and the sober with all their silly notions.

And then to punctuate their merriment
At its gayest height they tossed their tankards out
The window and where in the unkempt night they went
Gave not a fig but raised a happy shout.

One tankard was forever lost and gone.
The other into a sleeping piglet turned
And I saw it there where I stood in the dark alone
And to keep it for my own most yearningly burned.

I seized it by a trotter and tucked it to me
And felt it nestle with its tail a-twirling
And thought the piglet was a friend that knew me
While it sang in its sleep like ragged bagpipes skirling.

THE WILD SEVENTH PART

Divide humanity into seven parts,
Let's say, and see if everyone will fit.
First come Commanders who tell us all
Everything we ought to think and do;
Then come the Aesthetes stricken with the arts,
Quarreling like blue macaws in the zoo;
The Torpid simply do not give a shit;
The Holy-Woolies believe they hear a call
From God Who tells them what they do is right—
Whatever it is they do—and shall be blest;
The Hotjox think combat in sport is best
Of all the world affords by day or night;
The Smirkers consider everything a jest
In which the others take an interest.

That leaves the zany seventh part, the Dancers
To Bagpipes and Kissers of Piglets, and I include
Myself among them, having more tunes than answers,
And drinking wine whenever I'm in the mood.

This silly seventh part the world doesn't need, I'm told;
Its weight remains the same with the fraction subtracted.
In fact, it heavies a bit and looks rather old
And mumbles to itself, blank and abstracted.

And that's because this seventh is the leavening
That adds a yeasty commotion and a kiss
Of lightness to the lump that otherwise
Would sink to leaden oblivion in the abyss.
This seventh part is like a silver string
Attaching the duller mass to sun-blue skies.

THE SILVER STRING

Easy to mistake for a fleet star-beam—
But if you measure the apex angle that fixes
The pole by Polaris and parts the parallaxes

And makes the sky flow clear as a mountain stream,
You find it is the string of a dulcimer,
A silver string in length as infinite
As cross-eyed human confusion. A hammer
Of solar wind strikes it continually
And makes it chime and drone so glad all night
That on the land below and on the sea
The queen in her court, the tars in their galleon,
Gigue and gavotte and tipple the honeyed wine,
The wine that was wrung all ruby from the moon.

THE MOON'S WINE RED AND WHITE

In October the moon goes ruby and its light
Obliterates the stars about the sky.
Plump cloudlets cluster raceme-like as they float,
Dusted over, as if with must, all pinkish gray.

Then are launched the sky-trawlers one by one;
They cast their webs of platinum filament
To harvest the clouds all rosy and tumescent
As a snood gathers the copper hair of a woman.

Vast vats receive them, nearly as big as seas,
Where they're stirred and squished and pounded like a drum
Till each roseate cloud of superfluities
Is distilled to a drop of wine that befriends the cerebrum.

> *O now I wish it was scarlet October*
> *And I was drinking the ruby-moon wine*

The moon in December comes down white and hard
And covers the ground with a clinking hoarfrost luminance
That thickens to diamonds and other classy brilliants,
Each facet coruscant and uniquely starred.

In black chamois boots the rakers with long rakes
Garner the shingle that rattles like dice on a tombstone

And trundle it to the giant crusher that makes
A sound like a cow wild-eyed in sugar cane.

This scintillant powder is mingled in water until
It kindles to a frolic champagne as keen
As the handy executioner's swift-flashing steel
And silver as the shining oceans of the moon.

> *O don't I wish it was nippy December*
> *And I was sipping the filigree vintage*

DON'T I WISH

I had an old wish in the shape of a horse
And every St. Stephen's Day at noon
I donned the costume of a purblind mendicant
And spurred my steed over the flint roadstone
Until the populace, singing in chorus,
With coins of gold and sapphires jubilant
Pelted me so from every side
That I dismounted, sat down, and cried.

SIT DOWN AND WEEP

A good hard cry is as real as money.

The Maestro of Carouses practices
An elegant economy. He has
Four daughters each as lovely as an ocean
Wave when it collapses its vertical motion
To a horizontal strand of pearl and lace.

But women may be sad, though comely of face,
If no lion-heart knight appear. The daughters four
Sit on plush and weep and when their brazen ewer
Is full of earnest tears they flavor them
With rose attars as rare as Château d'Yquem
And freeze them to ice on the moonblown snowy hill.
Then when the ballroom heats with waltz and quadrille
These icy tears are served as delicacies
To the stalwart waltzers and flirtatious waltzees.

Didn't I tell you the Maestro knows
A thing or two
About the saving up of money and the constancies
Of woe?

THE WOEFUL DAUGHTERS
OF THE MAESTRO

I think of the women who are the brides
Of sorrow and think their presences
Ennoble this swaggering world that abrades
Their hearts with priceless bitterness.

I think this world can never deserve
The dignity and fortitude
That each of them lends to her travail,
The solemnities of her solitude.

The world, I fear, is so numberless
It never adds up to make a whole.

THE SUM OF IT ALL
IS LESS THAN A WHOLE

O fragile friends of mine, my piebald clowns
And motley jongleurs and silent saintly Pierrots,
When I perch on an alp and look across the towns,
The seas and harbors, the hills with mauve shadows,
Cathedrals spire on spire, and marketplaces,
The wars and truces, money changing hands
Relentlessly, the oceans of alarming faces,
The widows, the maimed and oozy hospitals weeping,
The pleasant grounds where the fertile dead lie sleeping,
And all the darkened and enlightened lands
So fearfully busy with their self-regard—
I begin to think our chosen life is hard
Because it is no more than a brief phantasm
Flitting the brains of tipplers merry and old
The way a butterfly traverses a chasm
Gloomy and vertiginous and cold

As permafrost. The Maestro of Carouses
And his tacit friend the Impresario
Of Moons are snoozing equally noisy snoozes,
And when they wake, all tremble-kneed and sober,
And vow that *Never again: the party is over,*
Perceiving the world as sour eructative data,
We'll all be canceled as being mere silly errata.

A RAY OF HOPE

But it's possible (as I prefer to think)
They'll open one red eye and call for drink,
Finding this cankered world not worth the trouble
It costs to manage clarity of thought.
—Then we'd persist, like a diamond champagne bubble,
Forever, twanging our tunes as we best know we ought.

Moonswarm

Tonight the telescope allows us to see
The Moonswarm drifting through the black midnight.
Soft creatures, neither giant moths
Nor fairies, they wheel their multitudinous light
Above the sleeping landscape. They sound and then withdraw
A singing as of many mouths
Like the mosquito's sostenuto saw
Multiplied a thousand times.
They constitute a soaring choir
Of peony-petal voices, a cottony fire
Made up of separate singing flames.

We cannot find if they are sentient,
These flocks that often obscure
The stars with their snowflake shine.
It seems that they appear
Only when the moon is absent
From the sprinkled skies,
And this has led some scholars to believe,
Or maybe only to surmise,
That our full moon is but the hive
Of the Moonswarm, where they nestle
As upon a great hydrangea blossom
The way a sleepy child will nuzzle
Closer within the mother's bosom.

If not this, then what are they?
We only know—we say
We only think we know—
That their migrations regulate
The ebb and subtle flow
Of dreams that tincture the complots of the rational State
With a phosphor glow.

What do they feed on? How reproduce?
The single theory that carries any weight
Says,
They feed on nothing and they do not mate.

So then, they cannot exist.
Demonstrably they still do,
Like half the objects in this world that halfway are:
On one side of their being, stone;
On the other, mist:
Mostly sheer fantasy and yet mostly true,
Like the mathematic particles that comprise a star.

Tonight the telescope discloses
These pale ephemerae,
Palpable impalpable animals,
As partly substantial as you and I.

Rider

for Heather Miller

In the viburnum thicket by the midnight lake
Twelve naked children huddle and murmur
As the wind strokes the invisible leaves.
Sad patience has overtaken them,
Their eyes are dark and liquid.

At last the rider comes. It is Night
On his cloud-gray stallion, his black cloak
Billowing behind him voluminous as a schooner
Full of stars. He makes no sound;
The hooves of his mount come down silent as dew.

When he stops in the broad and leaf-strewn path,
The children come out and climb up behind him.
They hold each other tight.
Away they go then to the place near and dim and far,
The palace where happiness is.

And these, so I am told, are the facts of the case,
Just the way they happened.

All the fairy tales really happened, you know,
All the fairy tales are true.

All except our own.

Narcissus and Echo

Shall the water not remember   *Ember*
my hand's slow gesture, tracing above   *of*
its mirror my half-imaginary   *airy*
portrait? My only belonging   *longing*
is my beauty, which I take   *ache*
away and then return as love   *of*
of teasing playfully the one being   *unbeing.*
whose gratitude I treasure   *Is your*
moves me. I live apart   *heart*
from myself, yet cannot   *not*
live apart. In the water's tone,   *stone?*
that shining silence, a flower   *Hour,*
whispers my name with such slight   *light,*
moment, it seems filament of air,   *fare*
the world become cloudswell.   *well.*

The Story

for Barbara Moran

Once upon a time the farmer's wife
told it to her children while she scrubbed potatoes.
There were wise ravens in it, and a witch
who flew into such a rage she turned to brass.

The story wandered about the countryside until
adopted by the palace waiting maids
who endowed it with three magic golden rings
and a handsome prince named Felix.

Now it had both strength and style and visited
the household of the jolly merchant
where it was seated by the fire and given
a fat gray goose and a comic chambermaid.

One day alas the story got drunk and fell
in with a bunch of dissolute poets.
They drenched it with moonlight and fever and fed it
words from which it never quite recovered.

Then it was old and haggard and disreputable,
carousing late at night with defrocked scholars
and the swaggering sailors in Rattlebone Alley.
That's where the novelists found it.

Pierrot Escapes

1

He floats. The triple gibbet of Cytherea
Flees into gray distance. The tufted clouds
Graze like salmon-colored sheep in the blue
And sunless sky. Below him, prairies of mandolins

Glitter like oceans of porcelain marguerites,
Their song a smoky echo. Pierrot is busy
With his ropes and gauges, pensive
As ever, a pale interior man. The world

He leaves behind, all that pastoral badinage,
He begins to remember in the way that one recalls
The scent of the crushed clover of childhood.
His balloon sways him like a pendulum.

2

Far from the carnival of noble hearts, he wanders
Shining like a butterfly, far
From the fresh and fragile brilliance, that light
Transforming folly into figures of a dance.

The sky surrounds him with its fretful angels
Of whom he takes no notice. *O my sisters,*
What was it all about, that life petite
And nougat? The chandeliers are falling,

The ivied garden tiers collapse, an avalanche
Of frou-frou buries the searching mind.
Pierrot, balloonist and philosopher, considers
His escape with a lonely satisfaction. No more,

3

No more of that forever. *Untie the garter ribband
Of society.* Farewell farewell
The coifed spaniel and bal masque. Pierrot's balloon
Rises among the stars like a wedding cake.

He travels to farther worlds. On Mars, perhaps,
Or Jupiter, live races more to his desire:
Savages with easy hearts, sans malice, envy, fear,
Who have not learned the poison compliment.

The Tipsy Diva Remembers Pierrot

He sent no billets-doux or flowers
When he set out to win my love.
To amuse my sullen hours
He brought a single velvet glove.

A glove as small as any leaf
From the young and lissome willow tree,
A glove as dark as Tristan's grief
For his Iseult beyond the sea.

The glove was sewn as cunningly
As a sonata by Telemann
And joyed my sense with such beauty
That I determined to try it on.

I laid it gently on the floor
And crept into it. And you should know
That it was warm as the underwear
Of any arctic Eskimo.

And who awaited me inside?
Who else but ardent Pierrot?
And there we lived a long decade,
Trading kisses blow for blow.

Then came a bitter killing frost,
Then darkened all the land with snow.
Our little glove gave up the ghost;
And so did precious Pierrot.

Now I am ghostly too and wander
Like a lost adagio,
And people stare at me and wonder
What life was like with Pierrot.

Epigrams

The rose is valued for its gorgeous blossom,
    Watercress for its leaf;
The ode embodies noble resonance,
    The epigram is brief.

Going Through Zero to the Other Side

Let's get down to the point.

Pulled like a noodle through Omega's aperture,
I emerge smaller than any possible size.

Yet this side of the nought looks exactly like the other:
a flat blank boring colloidal tympanum.

I had figured, *Once there it will be different,*
it will be completely imaginary.

But it is only the simple same turned over—
only now I face the sunset.

Fleurs-des-Livres

It rained through my window forgotten open
On my books of poems. They sprouted like potato eyes.
What a clutch of impulse, groping
For sunlight! Those tubers iridescent as ice.

Whitman came up kudzu and sawbriar,
Vines hairy and rough and muscular,
Stretching to wrestle manfully
Mr. Eliot's pallid celery.

Miss Moore's snowdrops glittered chirping
Beneath Laforgue's sardonic moon
Flower. The Bukowski-worts were burping.
Dickinson sprang forth bare bone.

Pope's natty tulips rank on rank.
The Roethke reseeding itself again,
Wallowing belly-deep in my dank
Library, snuffling like a hog in the rain.

And swaying above this unweedable plot
Blake's infirm Rose towered tall as the trees,
And there roared from the heart of this polyglot
A clamor like Pindar's apostrophes.

Upon a Confessional Poet

You've shown us all in stark undress
The sins you needed to confess.
If my peccadilloes were so small
I never would undress at all.

No Defense

"'Even Homer nods,' you said;
You've said it many times before.
It won't apply in your case, Fred.
He doesn't pass out cold and snore."

Literary Critic

Blandword died, and now his ghost
Drifts gray through lobby, office, hall.
Some mourn diminished presence; most
Can find no difference at all.

Another

Blossom's footnotes never shirk
The task of touting his own work.

Another

Procrustes kept a Theory as a pet
And fed it all the verses he could get.
One day it swallowed down a bona fide
Poem, fell ill, turned blue, and died.
He got it stuffed and keeps it on display,
Pleased to see it worshiped every day.

Rx

Dr. Rigsbee
Drank all my whiskey.
He said, when I objected, "Hell,
Fred, you're paying me to make you well."
—Martial

Upon an Amorous Old Couple

This coltish April weather
Has caused them to aspire
To rub dry sticks together
In hopes that they'll catch fire.

U.S. Porn Queen (Ret.)

The years alas have been unkind
To every part except her mind;
That organ too seems to betray
More insidiously every day.

She cannot now recall just who
Her partners were in all that blue,
The hapless women, reckless men
Directors smeared upon her skin.

Those charms once bared for all to see
Are subject now to gravity;
The passing years amass to seal
In gravure all her sex appeal.

Her peachy wares no longer viable,
She finds vocation in the Bible.
Chaste as Diana, rich as Croesus,
She locks her knees and thinks of Jesus.

Sex Manual

We've followed instructions to the letter,
Pausing at diagram 82.
"Aren't we there yet?" one of us pleads,
But in this position I can't tell who.

Epitaph: Lydia

She enjoyed making love
In any exotic location.
Now Lydia lies here.
It's not the first occasion.

Threads

Listen, buddy, I knew you when
You were a man like other men,
Not on your high horse, puffed with pride,
But genial, friendly, bona fide.

Now you think you're a different breed
Because you wear expensive tweed
And flash the label that declares it.

But a sheep first wore it. A sheep still wears it.

Satire

Not to write satire is hard,
Said Juvenal. But the ancient chorus
Is silenced; Aristophanes
And Terence now go quite unheard,
Their lines too moderate to please:
The morning headlines write our satire for us.

The Epigrammatist

Mankind perishes. The world goes dark.
He racks his brain for a tart remark.

Poems of Memory

The sky appears, above the roof,
    Calm and blue.
The chestnut sways, above the roof,
    To and fro.

The church bell through a patch of sky
    Distantly rings.
A bird within that patch of tree
    Plaintively sings.

O God O God, all life lies there
    In tranquil ease;
The murmurs of the city are
    Soft on the breeze.

—What have you done, unhappy man,
    To weep such tears?
What have you done, unhappy poet,
    With your young years?

So wrote Paul Verlaine in his prison cell
After the idiocy of *l'affaire Rimbaud;*
So wretched now his memory would allow
His past to confront him only as a hell
His bully friend more deeply understood.
The case is less uncommon than we suppose
Who sugar over our pasts with all the good
We did. We did so much—and no one knows!

Both these casts of memory—the phony,
The tortured—are deleterious alike
In their effects upon us who must take,
Or try to take, each day that comes as a lonely
Only, not forgetting the plenitude
Of errors that made us partly what we are,
Yet still determined to stand against the flood
Of present time, its famine, terror, war,

Its swift betrayals, proud hypocrisies,
The lies that pass for canny politics,
The theft, the bribery, the dirty tricks,
The public that applauds these treacheries,
The cities that consume themselves with crime . . .
Well, I could list forever, but I won't;
God didn't lend me world enough and time,
As *carpe diem* ebbs to *ubi sunt*.

And if we undertake to reminisce,
As lifelong lovers may spend hours to do,
To sit and sip a thoughtful cup of tea,
The garden is a sweet superior place.
I like to think, in a fuzzy waking dream,
That such warm pleasure's not confined to man,
That other animals take up the theme—
That chickens may ask, "Où sont les neiges d'antan?"

THE UBI SUNT LAMENT OF THE BELDAME HEN

Is there no one who can tell
The tales of heroes of olden days,
Their voices strong as the chapel bell?
When they strutted their stuff on straw runways
Their plumage shed resplendent rays.
O where is noble Chanticleer
On whom the world adored to gaze?
Where are the cocks of yesteryear?

There was a rooster journeyed to hell,
Or so the ancient legend says,
Who conquered there and came back whole
To fill the world with strange amaze.
O Orpheus, in limp times like these
We need a champion who has no fear
To shame the devil to his face.
But where are the cocks of yesteryear?

Where are Hector and William Tell,
Veterans of a thousand frays?
Where is Ajax who never fell,
And had such polish, such winning grace,

He was the jewel of our race?
With eye so red and comb so rare,
His was the look that truly slays.
O where are the cocks of yesteryear?

This conundrum that I raise
Was broached of old by La Belle Heaulmière
In Master Villon's langue française:
Where are the cocks of yesteryear?

Susan, we've reached that mellow period
That offers a truly rare and curious pleasure:
We now look forward to looking back in leisure,
Fretting little the future present in God.
To fear the worst is not impiety,
Only a picklepuss ungraciousness
That adds no ornament to a happy day
And leaves a dreary day a turgid mess.

It's true that we begin to take precautions
As joints and sinews start to crack and creak
And intellectual powers grow kitten-weak
And social life avoids loud commotions.
But how can we regret a regimen
Enabling us to live as we had hoped
We someday would? We always had a plan,
One that evil years battered and scraped,

That now we resurrect as we approach
A time that makes it possible at last
To welcome Quiet as an honored guest
And listen to the poet Horace broach
Advice on how to spend the years to come.
He bids us not to worry, to drink some wine,
And in the lines that gave us "carpe diem"
Tells us to leave astrologers alone:

Let's not go prying, Susan, into forbidden
Knowledge; it's best our death-dates remain hidden
From any calculating astrologer.
This winter, with its stone-destroying power,

May be our last; or maybe several more
God has allotted us.
                        —Be wise. Drink up.
Our brief lives shorten, wasted in long hope.
Now while we chat, the light hours fleet away.
Credit no tomorrow. *Seize the day.*

How better seized than to remember when
Our love was new and we were full of fear
And any thought might start a secret tear
Or any frown transform into a grin?
There's not much fun in being mostly broke
At an expensive university,
And loony Fred was the most improvident bloke
To have to face such square adversity.

But we got by, through your deft management,
And read the books and wrote the dumb exams
And watched some friends go down in angry flames
While others settled in with sweet content.
My ambitions were to write poetry
And make a modest living teaching school,
Happy to suffer the Eighteenth Century
And week on week of tuna casserole.

—That's why I waste no precious cerebration
In choosing for our salad memory-herbage;
Too many years we spent in pinchpurse curbage—
It's time to pop the corks of celebration.
Let us accompany our choice greens
With freshbaked loaves of chewy Italian bread
And open a variety of wines,
A California white, a Spanish red,

A Provençal rosé, a light Bordeaux,
Perhaps a muscat from the upper Loire,
A German Riesling to lend its nimble air,
And one dark bottle of earthy staunch Margaux.
And on the side we'll set a plate of cheese:
Red Leicester, Roquefort, and an aged Cantal
If we can find it, several creamy Bries,
A runny Camembert with lots of soul.

These will make our salad memorable
For our anniversary déjeuner
Beneath our oak trees where the hastening day
Makes even mortal thoughts quite beautiful.
A skimpy dressing of oil and lemon juice—
A spackle of leaf-shadowed noonday sun—
Give the pepper mill three hearty screws—
And our spring garden salad is quite done.

Humility

In the necessary field among the round
Warm stones we bend to our gleaning.
The brown earth gives in to our hands, and straw
By straw burns red aslant the vesper light.

The village behind the graveyard tolls softly, begins
To glow with new-laid fires. The children
Quiet their shouting, and the martins slide
Above the cows at the warped pasture gate.

They set the tinware out on checkered oilcoth
And the thick-mouthed tumblers on the right-hand side.
The youngest boy whistles the collie to his dish
And lifts down the dented milk pail.

This is the country we return to when
For a moment we forget ourselves,
When we watch the sleeping kitten quiver
After long play, or rain comes down warm.

Here we might choose to live always, here where
Ugly rumors of ourselves do not reach,
Where in the whisper-light of the kerosene lamp
The deep Bible lies open like a turned-down bed.

A Prayer for the Mountains

Let these peaks have happened.

The hawk-haunted knobs and hollers,
The blind coves dense as meditation,
The white rock-face, the laurel hells,
The terraced pasture ridge
With its broom sedge combed back by wind:
Let these have taken place, let them be place.

And where Harmon Fork piles uprushing
Against its tabled stones, let the gray trout
Idle below, its nervous plectrum a shadow
That marks the stone's clear shadow.

In the slow glade where sunlight comes through
In circlets and shifts from leaf to fallen leaf
Like a tribe of shining bees,
Let the milk-flecked fawn lie unseen, unseeing.

Let me lie there too
And share the sleep
Of the cool ground's mildest children.

Seated Figure

Immense blind wind marching the grove,
Mauling the stolid house and thrusting
Its paw down the stone flue. The stove
Roared, stuffed with flame to bursting.

The dim grandmother crouched to her needle.
Her rocking chair tipped back and forth.
Slowly the house began to sidle
In the north wind scouring the leafless earth.

Even when blue snow swarmed fast
Against the pane and the light went gray
She gave no sign. The time was past
When she took notice of wind-fray.

The night hurtled upon the night.
The roof arose and flew; then gone
Like an owl gliding the spare light.
She plied her needle under the bone moon.

Abandoned Schoolhouse on Long Branch

The final scholar scrawls his long
Black name in aisle dust, licks the air
With his inquisitive double tongue,
Coils up in shadow of a broken chair

And dozes like the farmer boys
Who never learned the capital
Of Idaho, found out the joys
Of long division, or learned what all

Those books were all about. Most panes
Are missing; the web-milky windows
Are open to the world. Dust grains
Swirl up and show which way the wind blows.

K. B. + R. J., cut deep
In a childish heart on the cloakroom wall.
Now Roger and Katherine Johnson sleep
Long past the summons of the morning bell.

The teacher sleeps narrow too, on yonder
Side of Sterling Mountain, as stern
With her fate as with a loutish blunder
In a Bible verse she'd set them to learn.

Sunset washes the blackboard. Bees
Return to the fluent attic nest
Where much is stored. Their vocalese
Soothes the patient golden dust.

Child in the Fog

Did the ghosts watch my prayers when the strange
Fat hats of everything attacked?
Or was it the fearful Nobody?
From the silent creek, glories of wet gauze.
The pigeons curled up in fists and mourned to me.

I began to know how
The Hour Without Eyes is gathering in the world.

The barn's hard lines went fuzzy;
Rafters dissolved to spirit;
The mice in the loft muttered warm dreams.
The gray tin roof wept an old woman's tears.

This was the rapture of humility which kept saying,
You are a child, you are suitable to be awed.
I heard the whole silence.
My heart went white.

It was the first day of school and They
Had betrayed me to the white fog leopard,
Tree-croucher to crunch my bones.
I crept to first grade like an opossum.
Afterward, the fog was my comforting cool sleep;
I could walk unseeable.
Not even the ghosts could be sure where I'd been.

Today I will build a fire the fog will clasp.
Childhood will burn in the grate and the white smoke
Will go out friendly to the cotton world.
All that I feared will attenuate in mist,
Muffling in hush the dripping hills,
And the other lost children, and the one lost child.

Nocturne

The black horse lifts its head and quivers
Its glossy shoulder. Powder of stars
Upon the autumn sky. A wind
Springs up and shakes bare flame-oak limbs
Across the primitive constellation.
An emery of frost on the slant fields.

An old man trudges the midnight road,
Bearing a totesack over his shoulder,
Bearing away in steady silence
All the breath of country sleepers.

Something small and trembling emerges
From the pond and seeks its leaf-meal burrow.
The stars creep back over the water.

And then the
one
bellchime of moonrise.

Message

for David Slavitt

True:
      the first messenger angel may arrive
purely clothed in terror, the form he takes
a swordblade of insuperable energies,
making the air he entered a spice of ozone.

And then, the mad inventories. Each trait
of nature, each animal and flower and pretty bird,
is guilty of persistence. The tear of sorrow,
huge as an alien star, invades
our sun's little system.

           Irrelevant,
such enormity: because the man is alone
and naked. Even the tenuous radiations
of the marauding star crush him like falling timbers.
The worst is, he must choose among sorrows
the one that destroys him most.

But see how all changes in that hour.

He ascends a finer dimension of event, feels with senses
newly evolved the long horizons unknown till now.
He is transformed head to foot, taproot to polestar.
He breathes a new universe, the blinding whirlpool
galaxies drift round him and begin to converse.

Cathedral

Notre Dame de Paris. Triple rose that enfolds
The mutter of hundreds as one might cup in his palm
The sound of bees, each buzz like the trembling silent
Overtone of a plucked wire. The arches are echoes
Seized in stone, stone vaulting skyward until the vaults
Are only echoes the eye hears within a haze of stone.

Our effable emotions live longest: yearning
And regret mark the hardest outlines against the clouds.
These are the shapes of prayers murmured and whispered,
Vault after vault in the long grove of columns, whisper
Of prayer drawn with a sound like silk across a leaf-edge,
Je suis desolée, Ave Maria plena gratia: the murmur
Like the wind that pierces the eyelet buttresses.

Avignon and Afterward

1. You

This day like the others cannot be seized.

The wineglass casts a circle of green shadow
On the liquid page, the page to be written
And unwritten, the page that remembers the fountain,
The moss and pink begonias, these ancient sycamores,
The waiter's childhood scattered through fourteen nations,
The massive gates with iron fleurs-de-lys.

After the autumn, after the first November snow,
You shall not remember it was Avignon,
Only that you had loved so much, so truly,
And were young no longer and loved the better
Because of that. And yet it might have been in Avignon
That these thoughts addressed themselves to you,
Asking you with steady demeanor never to forget.

2. Never

We have gazed at one another, Death, and never spoken.
One by one you take those whom I have loved
And leave a barren History. Over the towers
Of Avignon the dawn is pierced with swallows;
The walls brighten, the streets begin to mutter.
Under the bridge of Avignon the lovers
In their sleeping bags turn and turn again
As the sunlight crosses the Rhone, the traffic rouses.

I am afraid to die. You understand
I am afraid to die and so take many
I have loved to lend me courage by example.
It is terrible to see fine women die
Before I die. The bells peal one by one.
Each stroke counts one taken whom I have loved.
I know already that today
I shall look at you again and fail to speak.

3. In the Future

North out of Avignon into the cypresses and poppies,
Past the silver vineyards and the fields of lavender,
Along the Rhone under the mountain that birthed the Renaissance,
The train gathers speed and squanders it.
The villages flutter and settle again like butterflies.

Perhaps we shall return to Avignon and its poetry
Chaste and renowned. Perhaps the future holds it waiting,
This town, to be discovered like a dance card,
The one with the gold tassel and elegant engraving,
Mustily scented with lavender sachet,
The card your grandmother kept in the velveteen box
Until she died and you were old enough to understand.

Heath at Two: Learning to Talk

Three words he's linked together now
With sounds that are not words. Immense
The furrow of his candid brow
As babble troubles into sense.

Some toys he mothers. The silent stare
That is their mien can anger him
Or bore him into blank despair.
Too bad, when things just stay the same,

Worse when they don't. However kindly
He may ponder his stuffed kangaroo
Or cuddle his soiled monkey blindly—
He'll rage and tear off his doll's shoes:

Because objects won't talk. He is
A stranger in the world he's made
Out of his own fierce mind. He tries
To rule it, but he finds it mad.

In time he'll give these toys a tongue,
Pose them debating in his head;
Wild histories will fire among
These figures impudently dead.

But now the silence will not break.
He cannot find the awkward key
That opens their hush to let it speak,
Speak, speak—and set his loving free.

Afternoons with Allen

He'd smiling admit, with M. Teste,
"Stupidity is not my long suit." Then
Intently turn his pale pale eyes upon
Lombardi's Redskins mauling the TV screen.

"It's their precision I like, like a machine,"
He said, "like well-made poetry." And when
They lost he didn't much appear to care,
But chuckled at the unimportant score.

"Kicking is still part of the game. I'm glad."
He took a sip of meditative bourbon
And lit a cigarette. "Please don't tell Helen
I've been smoking."
                        (We didn't, but felt we should.)

Like Homer's famous snowflakes his words drifted
In the brass October brunt of light. He lifted
And let fall his delicate hand of smoke
That winged, moth-hesitant, through all his talk.

Tracery, traceries . . . Sometimes there stood outlined
Before us features of a remembered friend.
"Hem thought we make love just so many times.
A hot youth means short rations at the end.

"Miss Stein I never liked, rude, ignorant,
And prejudiced. I always wondered why
No one saw through her. Toklas was merely
Sad. Pound's talent crumbled into rant.

"My southern friends have been the best to me
Even when we fell out." For Lombardi
He fetched out of that high magniloquent head
A sonorous telling line of the Second Aeneid.

Forsitan et, Priami fuerint quae fata, requiras?

Heath at Eight: New Drum Set

Little tub full of thump.
Now let's bomb everything.
Someone likes to plop
And simmer on the floor.
Nevermore nevermore nevermore nevermore.

O reach him a cymbal too
To ring like the crickets in the trees.
And. uh. big. bass. drum.
Slogging through boglands,
We never hear each other.

It's your parents' blood
You're rattling, kid,
Stirring pulp and marrow together.
Hammer hammer like barracks a-building.
Thunder thunder like brontosaur weather.

Forever Mountain

J. T. Chappell, 1912–1978

Now a lofty smoke has cleansed my vision.

I see my father has gone to climb
Lightly the Pisgah slope, taking the time
He's got a world of, making spry headway
In the fresh green mornings, stretching out
Noontimes in the groves of beech and maple.
He has cut a walking stick of second-growth hickory
And through the amber afternoon he measures
Its shadow and his own shadow on a sunny rock.
    Not marking the hour, but observing
The quality of light come over him.
He is alone, except what voices out of time
Swarm to his head like bees to the bee-tree crown,
The voices of former life as indistinct as heat.

By the clear trout pool he builds his fire at twilight,
And in the night a granary of stars
Rises in the water and spreads from edge to edge.
He sleeps, to dream the tossing dream
Of the horses of pine trees, their shoulders
Twisting like silk ribbon in the breeze.

He rises glad and early and goes his way,
Taking by plateaus the mountain that possesses him.

My vision blurs blue with distance,
I see no more.
Forever Mountain has become a cloud
That light turns gold, that wind dislimns.

This is continually a prayer.

Epilogue

All in all, it's been a day's fair work,
Selecting each poetic salad green,
Pruning surplusage, trimming the borders clean.
Now cool shadows begin to mass toward dark.
The garden tinges placid with evening light,
The slow sfumato pricked by fireflies
Like tiny intermittent stars in flight.
A thin mauve smoke tinctures the western skies.

Even the rasp of traffic dims a little,
Purling homeward on Walker Avenue;
Minute by minute the east darkens its blue;
Kitchen windows broadcast their tinware rattle.
Children at their swift games moderate
Their shouts and squeals, as if unconsciously
They recognize the hour is growing late
For youth as well as for maturity.

This is the murmurous time that gardens love,
When day-end breezes make their way across
The hedge, the thorn, the walks of emerald moss,
The centerpiece medallion with its grave
Beloved quotation from the Florentine
Who kept it lifelong in his mind until he
Came triumphant to the final line:
L'amor che muove il sole e l'altre stelle.

My life, I'm told, is one of privilege,
That I enjoy a leisure that amounts
To parasitism, that no existence counts
Which doesn't push hard purpose to the edge;
My happy studies in ancient poetry,
In French, in the Italian renaissance,
In science, religion, and philosophy
Are fusty hobbies that make no advance

In useful knowledge and contribute nought
To the urgent betterment of humankind,
That I should get off my sagging behind
And start to do the things I know I ought:

Like making sure that justice comes to women,
To all the beaten-down and needy races
Everywhere, including the nonhuman,
Until the pain in this universe ceases.

—Friends, I was there to march the picket line,
Answer mail, write propaganda for
Organizations against whatever war,
Carry petitions for sad converts to sign,
And now I'm willing to let someone else
Lick the stamps and trudge holes in their shoes,
Wear bumper stickers, and raise forty hells
About the latest horrors in the news.

It doesn't mean a thing if there's no heart.
Mine has given way to common sense.
Too many times it turned to violence,
That charity pursued with little art
And a stony lack of necessary patience.
In my garden, reading a poetry book,
No longer I influence the fate of nations;
Now they're on their own. I wish them luck.

Ronsard himself had to face down such taunts.
In his "Response aux Injures & Calomnies,"
He fully described for all the world to see
The nature of his life, his needs and wants,
His frugal habits and his studiousness,
His solitude and quiet benevolence,
Including his morning prayer for God to bless
His day to come, his country, and his Prince:

"Before anything else, when I arise from bed,
I invoke the Eternal Father, author of all good;
With humble heart I pray to Him to send His Grace,
That, without my offending, this newborn day shall pass;
That He keep me from error and dark religious strife
And help me live within my original belief;
That by no undertaking of thought or deed or word
I cause the least injury to my country or my lord."

Nor was Ronsard the only one to voice
Such bitter complaint. It was traditional
For poets to crab and carp, to mention all
The things in life that they did not find nice:
Chaucer's empty purse drew a ballade,
Skelton deplored the fact his times were changing,
Marot was always begging royal aid,
Villon seemed deeply to resent his hanging.

The scholar's life was the only life for them,
They said, although it kept them penniless,
Earned them but scorn in the common marketplace,
And made a willing woman a phantom dream.
But still they would be faithful to the Muse,
Pursuit of wisdom remain their avid work,
Even when they digressed to accuse
The mob—as in this sonnet by Petrarch:

"Greed, Ennui, and obese Luxury
Have driven from the world the better powers;
Sleazy habits have made us stray off-course
So that by now we've nearly lost our way.
The ancient lights of calm benignity
That used to guide mankind with gracious force
Have darkened; he who would restore such source
Is looked upon as a curiosity:

'What is he up to? What's his little game?
Philosophy and poetry? All right,
Then let him suffer with the deserving poor.'

So say the people; their leaders say the same.
But I say, Gentle Spirit, hold to the bright
Lonely path you've chosen forevermore."

It's good advice, Susan, but a hard act
To follow; sober precepts, noble thoughts
Shine in the mind until a toothache blots
Them out. Purpose shipwrecks on rocky fact;

Our sweet daybreak ideals founder by noon,
And we betray our best designs by three;
A world of cold disillusion the moon
Inspects with silent objectivity.

Most hang on to a slippery Ideal—
Sometimes described as hope in fancy dress.
It's only that we have such small success
Translating Mental into daily Real
That we become impatient with our thinkers
And swear they have nothing helpful to give,
Plowing the rutted furrows in heavy blinkers
Of the barren prospect we call Western Civ.

But if philosopher and poet never sat
Sorting salad greens and sipping wine
And puzzling out some weird cosmic design
In a quiet garden with a neighbor's cat,
Who knows if we'd find courage to rise from bed
And brew some coffee, skip our exercise,
Read the papers, make a livelihood,
And try new resolutions on for size.

Someone has to dream the dreams and write
Them out in the best language they can find
To inspire and decorate the restless mind;
Otherwise, the damn thing takes a blight.
It's in our nature to explore the sky,
The sea, Plato's theory of the Good,
The atom, the virus. *Tomorrow* is our cry:
"Tomorrow to brash moods and postures nude."

But let us end on an elegiac note:
If a garden is the place for poetry,
Its theme will be human mortality,
Whatever subjects it may talk about,
Including love, warfare, faith in God,
The silly tragic destiny of man.
Pierre Ronsard composed on his deathbed
A poem borrowed from the emperor Hadrian:

And I—*with thanks*—shall borrow it again:

To His Soul

O Chappellette, flimsy marionette,
    My precious trembling wet-eyed pet,
        Guardian of my every breath,
Down you go, silent, white,
    Without a scrap of coverlet,
        Into the cold Kingdom of Death,
Without remorse, without regret,
    Without the least concern for what
        You leave the greedy world to keep;
That Prize they strain so hard to get,
    With doubletalk and bloodstained sweat,
        Would cause the sunbaked sands to weep.

        Goodbye, my friends. The sun has set.
        Now I lay me down to sleep.

Notes

Readers may be curious to visit the originals of the translations and adaptations scattered through the various prologues and the epilogue. They are these:

Pierre de Ronsard: "Ma douce jouvance est passée," pages 4–5;
Charles d'Orléans, "Les fourriers d'été," 6;
Jean-Antoine de Baïf, "La rose est une belle fleur," 10;
Statius, "Jam trux ad Arctos," 26;
Ronsard, "Mignonne, allons voir si la rose," 37–38;
Emile Verhaeren, "Lorsque tu fermeras mes yeux," 38–39;
Charles Baudelaire, "Les Chats," 89;
Paul Verlaine, "Le ciel est, par-dessus le toit," 129;
Horace, *Odes,* I, xi, 132;
Ronsard, "Response de P. Ronsard, Gentilhomme Vandomois, aux Injures &
    Calomnies de je ne sçay quel Predicans & Ministres de Genève," 152;
Petrarch, "La gola e'l sonno e l'oziose piume," 153;
Hadrian, "Animula vagula, blandula," and Ronsard, "Amelette Ronsardelette," 155.

The ballade attributed to Donald Hall on pages 87–88 is occasioned by some of his comments in private correspondence and by his remarks about William Stafford as reported in the Raleigh *News & Observer,* June 12, 1994: "Stafford is a poet of ordinary life. He didn't find it necessary to become *maudit,* to follow Baudelaire to the whorehouse. . . . He got up at six in the morning in a suburb of Portland and drained the sump."